Billie Eilish
Happier Than Ever

ISBN 978-1-70514-321-6

Visit Hal Leonard Online at
www.halleonard.com

Contact us:
Hal Leonard
7777 West Bluemound Road
Milwaukee, WI 53213
Email: info@halleonard.com

In Europe, contact:
Hal Leonard Europe Limited
42 Wigmore Street
Marylebone, London, W1U 2RN
Email: info@halleonardeurope.com

In Australia, contact:
Hal Leonard Australia Pty. Ltd.
4 Lentara Court
Cheltenham, Victoria, 3192 Australia
Email: info@halleonard.com.au

GETTING OLDER

Words and Music by BILLIE EILISH O'CONNELL
and FINNEAS O'CONNELL

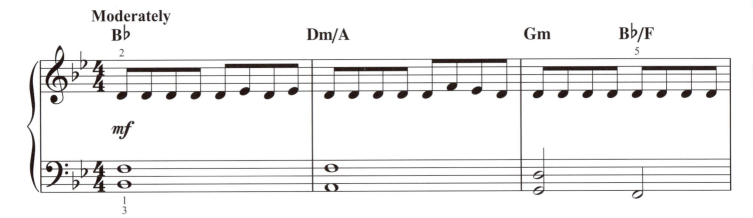

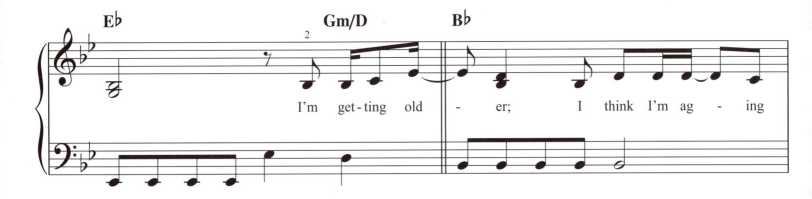

I'm get-ting old - er; I think I'm ag - ing

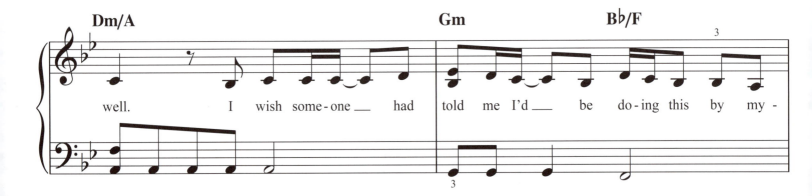

well. I wish some-one ___ had told me I'd ___ be do-ing this by my -

self. There's rea - sons that I'm thank - ful, there's a lot I'm grate - ful

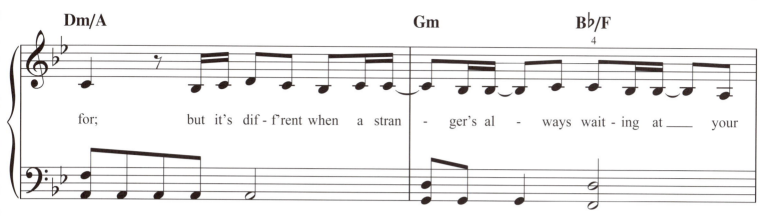

for; but it's dif - f'rent when a stran - ger's al - ways wait - ing at _____ your

door. Which is i - ron - ic, 'cause the stran - gers seem to want _

_ me more _ than an - y - one _ be - fore. (An - y - one be - fore.) _

Too bad _ they're u - sual - ly _ de - ranged. _

4

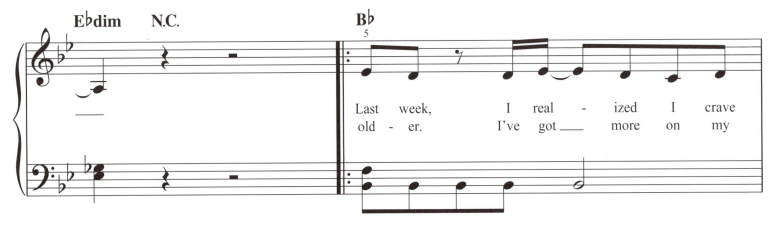

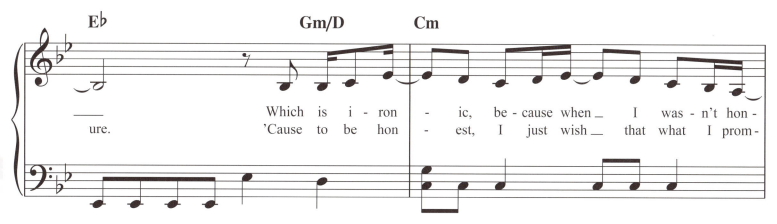

Which is i - ron - ic, be - cause when ___ I was - n't hon -
ure. 'Cause to be hon - est, I just wish ___ that what I prom -

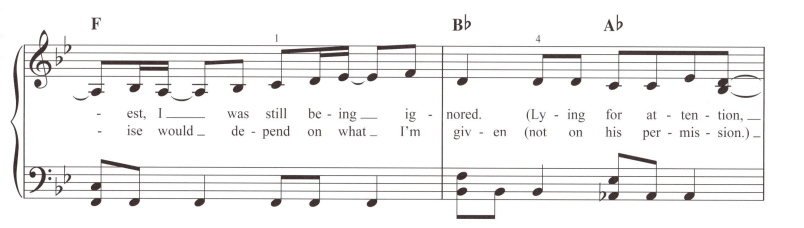

- est, I _____ was still be - ing ___ ig - nored. (Ly - ing for at - ten - tion,
- ise would ___ de - pend on what ___ I'm giv - en (not on his per - mis - sion.) ___

___ just to get ne - glect - tion.) ___ Now we're es - tranged. ___
___ Was - n't my de - ci - sion _____ to be a - bused. ___

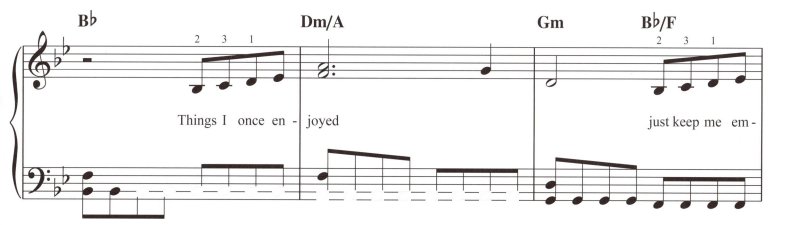

Things I once en - joyed just keep me em -

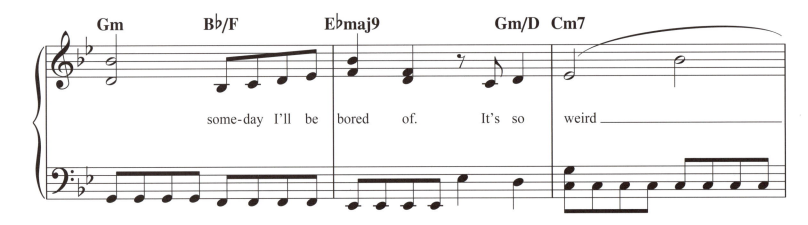

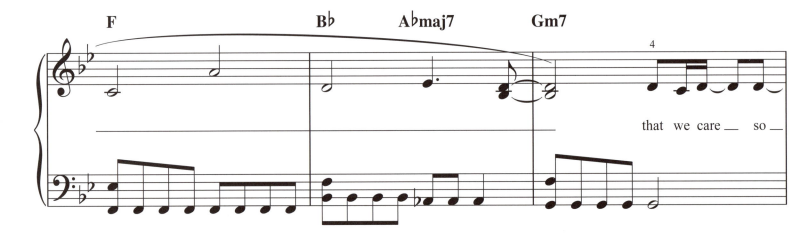

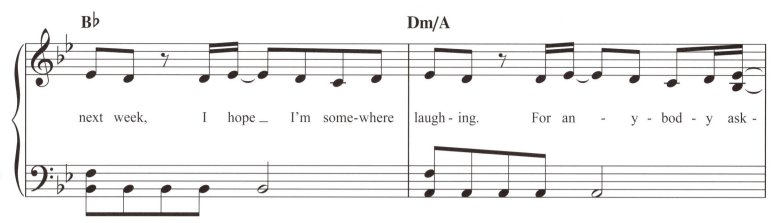

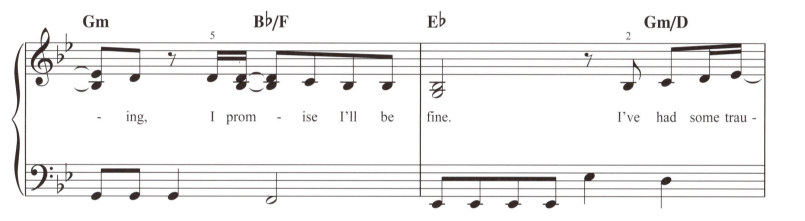

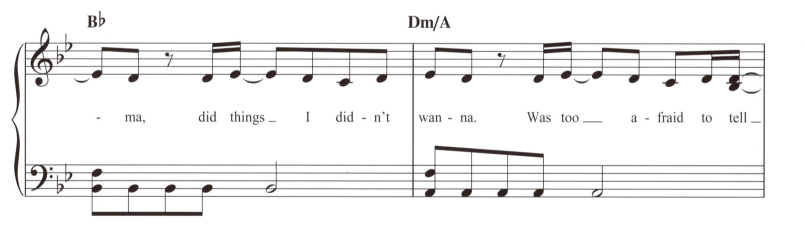

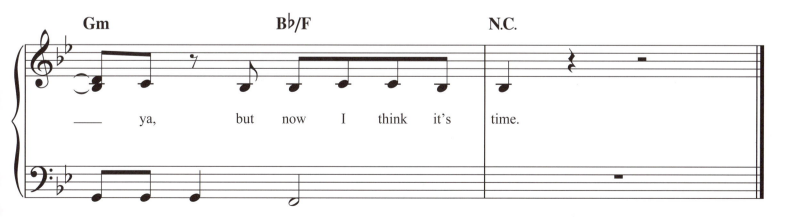

I DIDN'T CHANGE MY NUMBER

Slow Pop

Words and Music by BILLIE EILISH O'CONNELL
and FINNEAS O'CONNELL

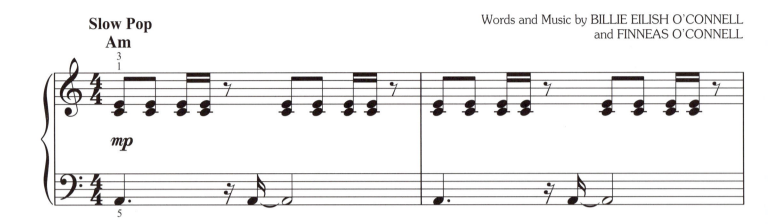

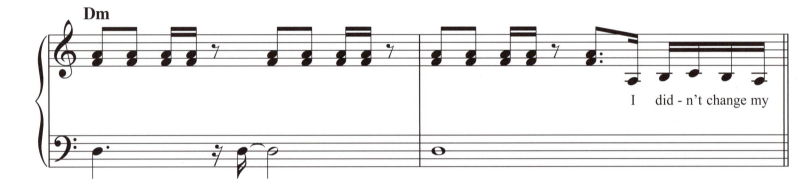

I did - n't change my

num - ber, I on - ly changed who I re - ply __ to. Lau - ra said I should be

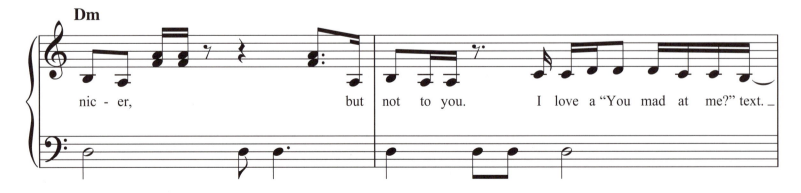

nic - er, but not to you. I love a "You mad at me?" text. __

Am

Should have guessed ___ that you would think I was up - set. ___

Dm

You're ob - sessed. ___ Don't take it

Am

out on me, I'm out of sym - path - y ___ for you. May - be

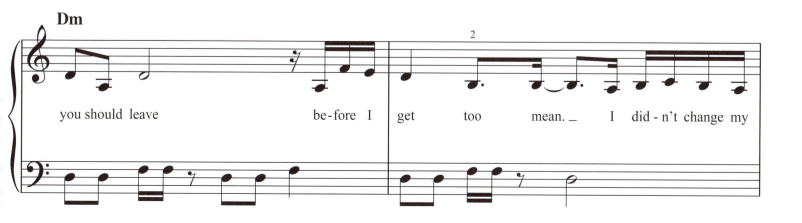

Dm

you should leave be - fore I get too mean. ___ I did - n't change my

Am

num - ber, I on - ly changed who I be - lieve _ in. You were eas - y on the

Dm

eyes, eyes, eyes, eyes, but looks can be de - ceiv - ing. I got - ta work, _

Am

_ I go to work, _ you don't de - serve _ to feel so hurt. You got a lot _

Dm　　　　　　　　　　　　　　　　　　　**Am**

_ of nerve, _ I don't de - serve _ so... Don't take it out on me, I'm out of

BILLIE BOSSA NOVA

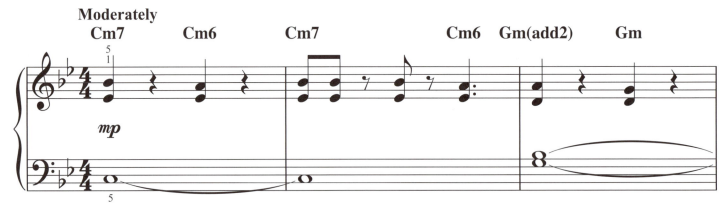

Words and Music by BILLIE EILISH O'CONNELL
and FINNEAS O'CONNELL

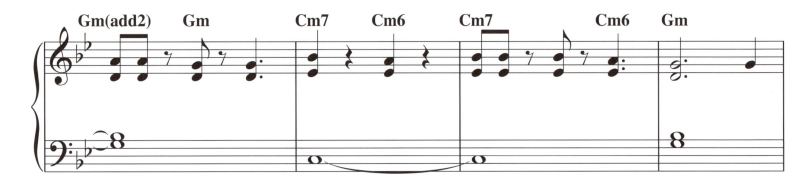

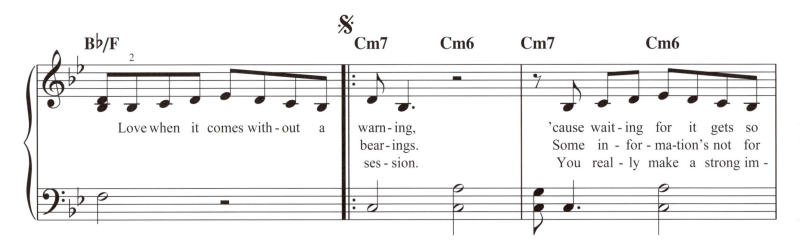

Love when it comes with-out a warn-ing,
bear-ings.
ses-sion.

'cause wait-ing for it gets so
Some in-for-ma-tion's not for
You real-ly make a strong im-

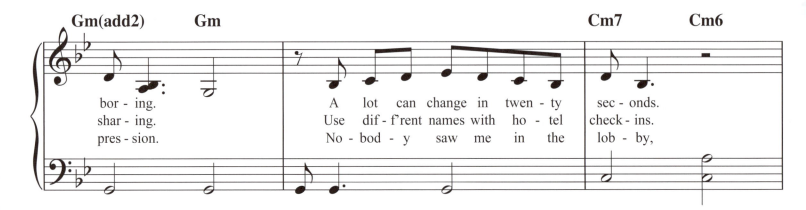

bor-ing.
shar-ing.
pres-sion.

A lot can change in twen-ty sec-onds.
Use dif-f'rent names with ho-tel check-ins.
No-bod-y saw me in the lob-by,

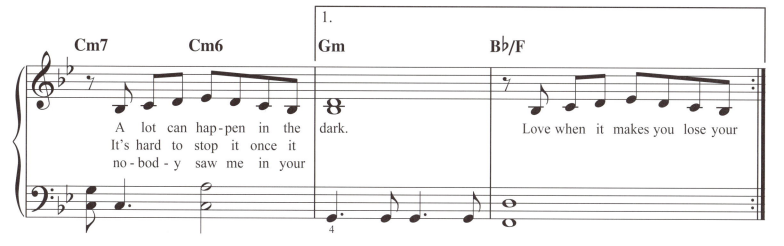

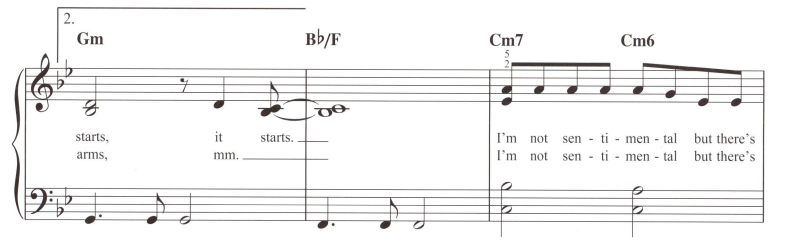

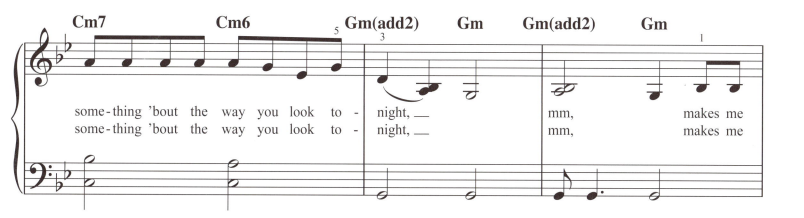

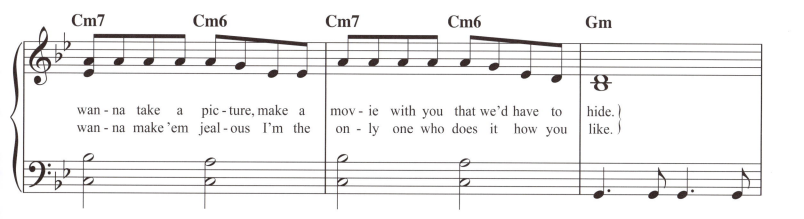

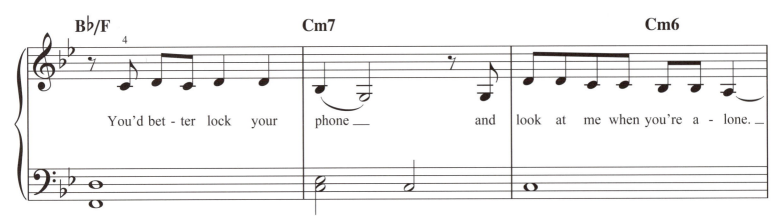

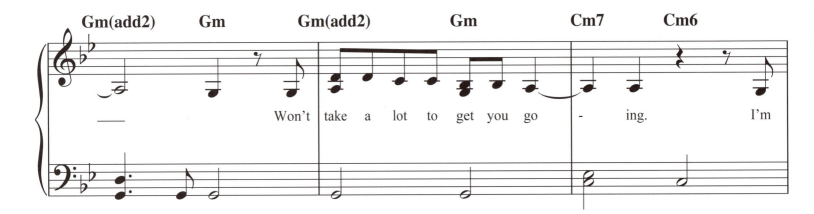

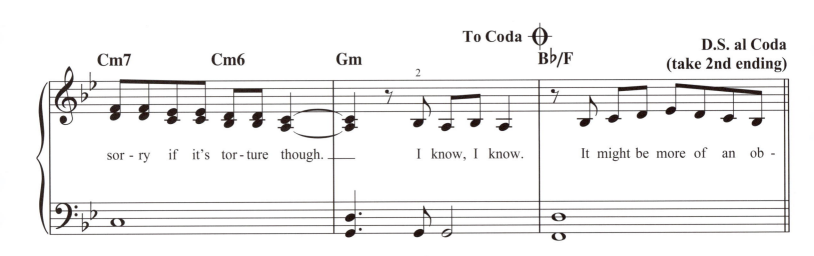

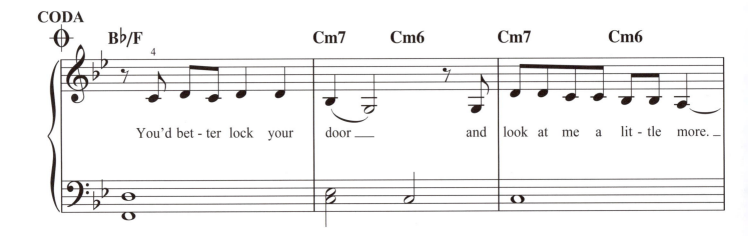

We both know I'm worth wait - ing for. ___ That

heav - y breath-ing on the floor. ___ I'm yours, I'm ___ yours. ___

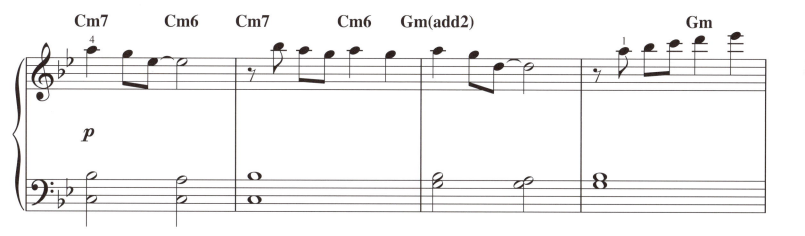

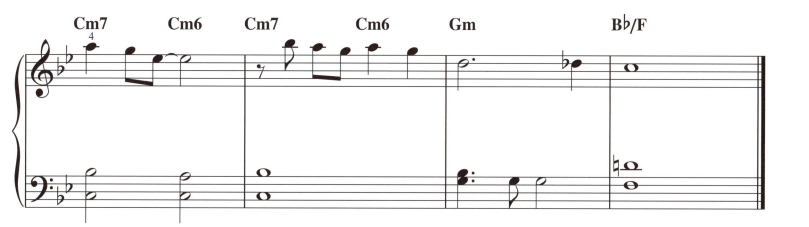

MY FUTURE

Words and Music by BILLIE EILISH O'CONNELL
and FINNEAS O'CONNELL

Slowly, in 2

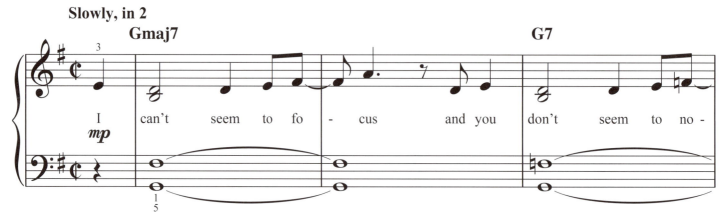

I can't seem to fo- cus and you don't seem to no-

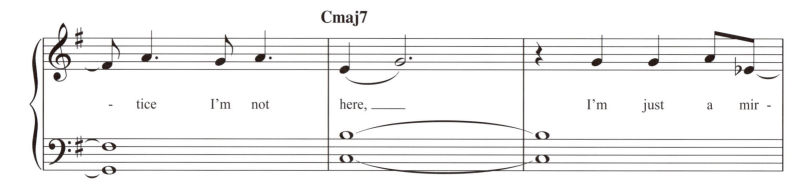

-tice I'm not here, _____ I'm just a mir-

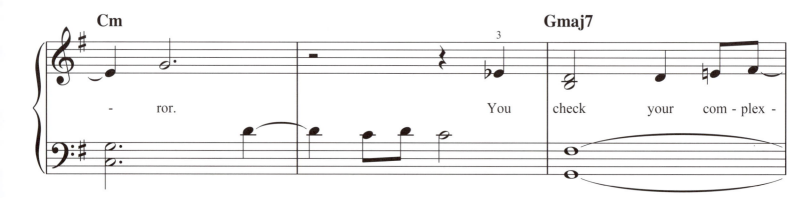

-ror. You check your com- plex-

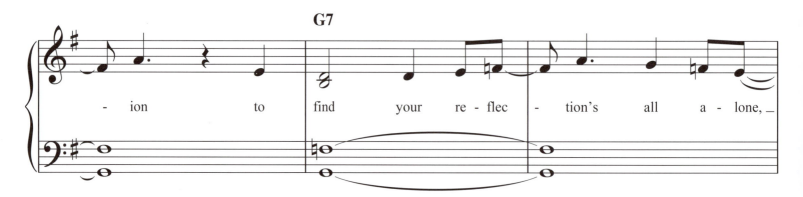

-ion to find your re- flec -tion's all a- lone, _____

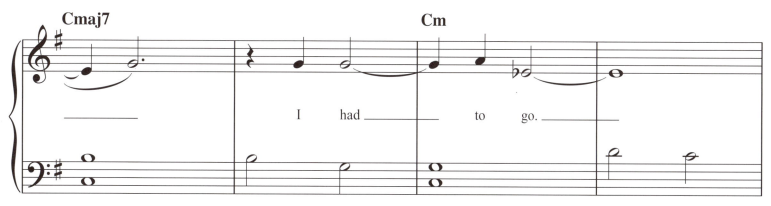

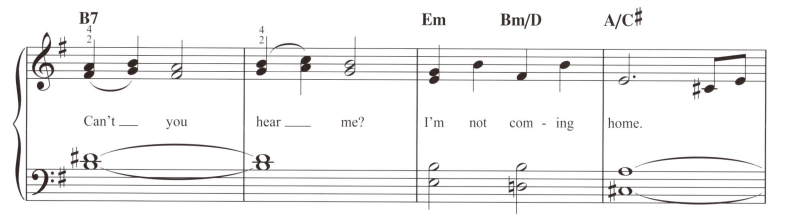

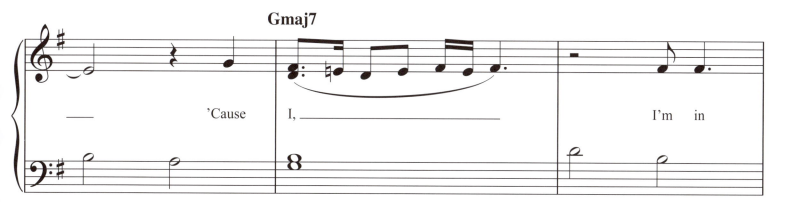

love _____ with my fu - ture, ___ can't wait to meet ___

_____ her. _____ And I, _____ I'm in

love _____ but not with an - y - bod - y else, ___

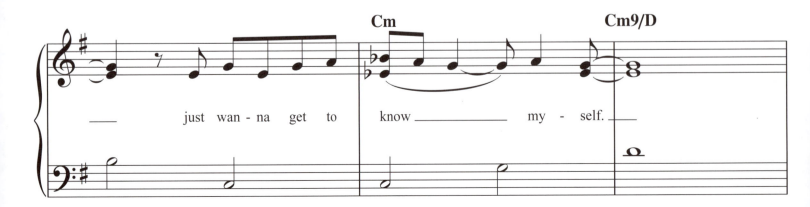

_____ just wan - na get to know _____ my - self. ___

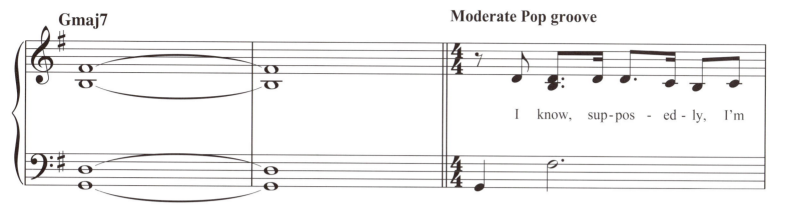

Gmaj7

Moderate Pop groove

I know, sup-pos - ed - ly, I'm

G7

lone - ly now, know I'm sup-posed to be un - hap - py with - out

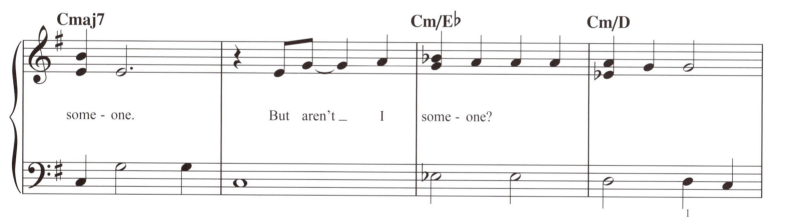

Cmaj7 **Cm/E♭** **Cm/D**

some - one. But aren't __ I some - one?

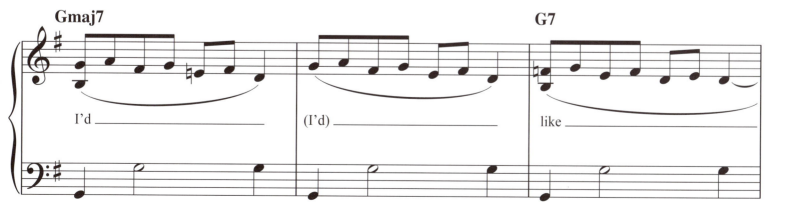

Gmaj7 **G7**

I'd __ (I'd) __ like __

Cmaj7

to be ___ your an - swer. 'Cause you're ___ so

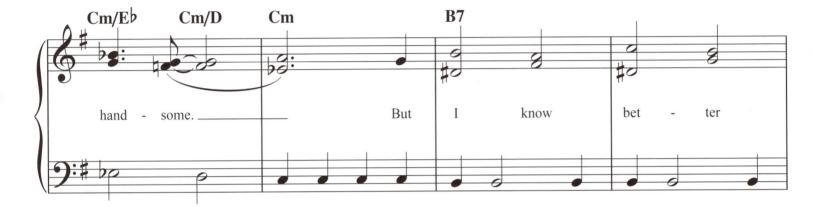

Cm/E♭   Cm/D   Cm   B7

hand - some. ___ ___ But I know bet - ter

Em   D   A/C♯   C

than to drive you home. 'Cause you'd in - vite me in ___

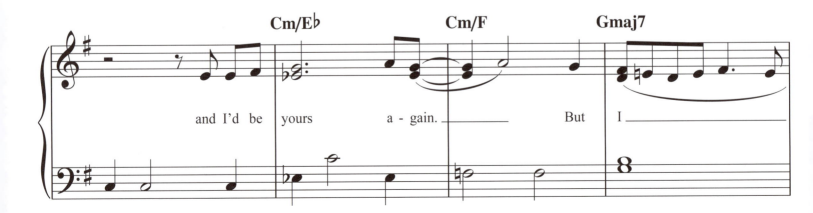

Cm/E♭   Cm/F   Gmaj7

and I'd be yours a - gain. ___ But I ___

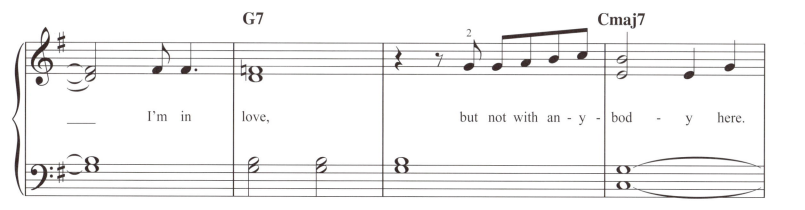

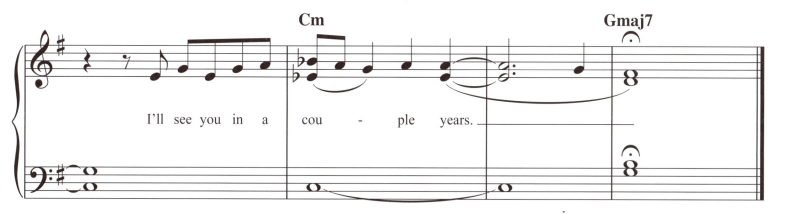

OXYTOCIN

Words and Music by BILLIE EILISH O'CONNELL
and FINNEAS O'CONNELL

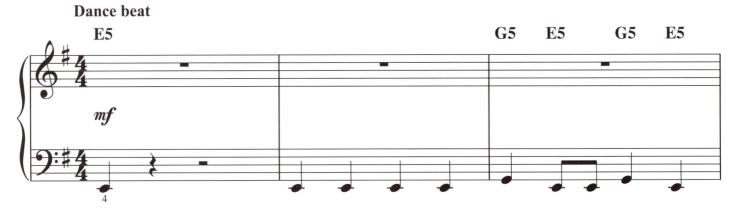

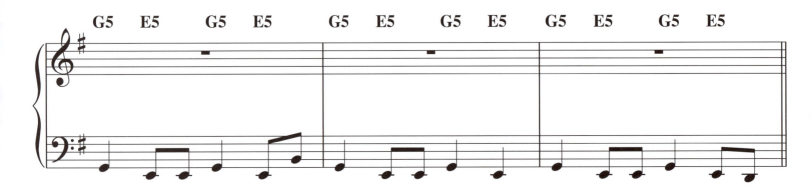

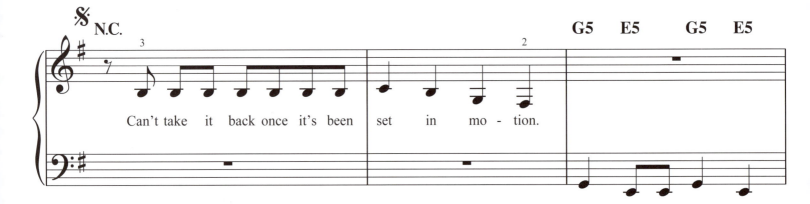

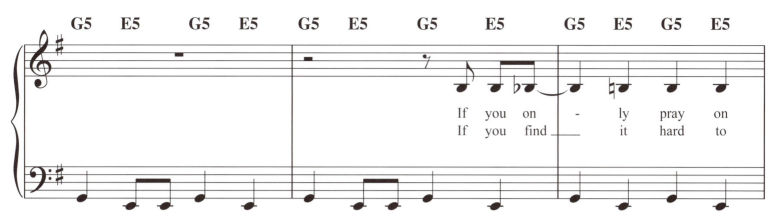

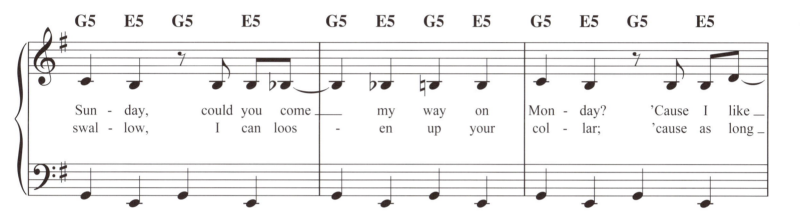

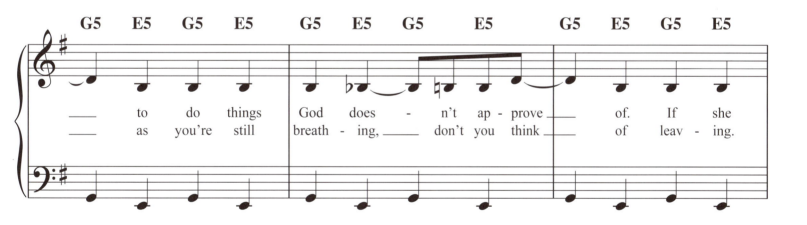

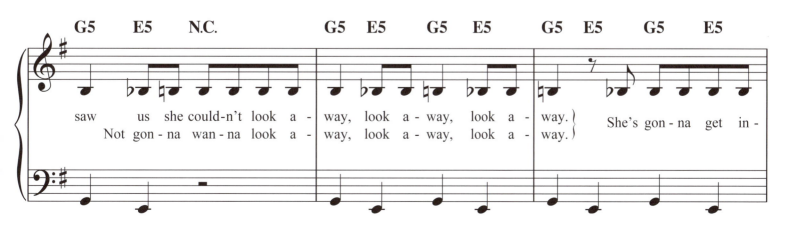

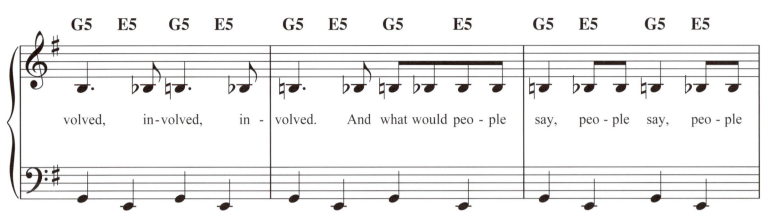

volved,   in-volved,   in - volved.   And   what would peo - ple   say,   peo - ple   say,   peo - ple

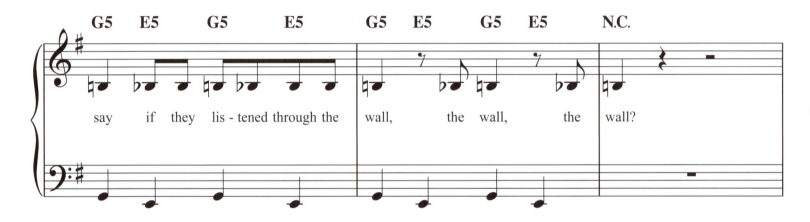

say   if they   lis - tened through the   wall,   the   wall,   the   wall?

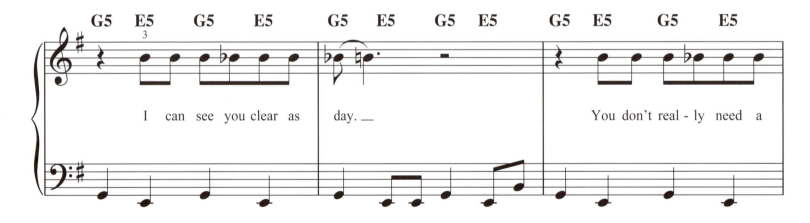

I   can see you clear as   day. __   You don't real - ly need a

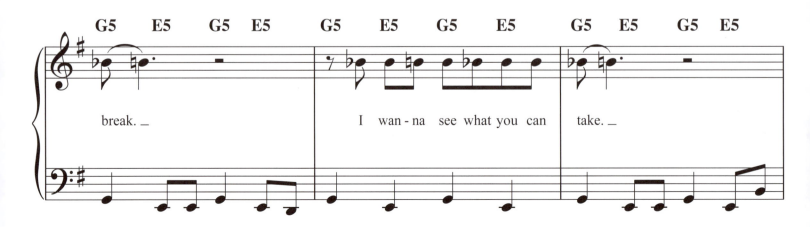

break. __   I wan - na   see what you can   take. __

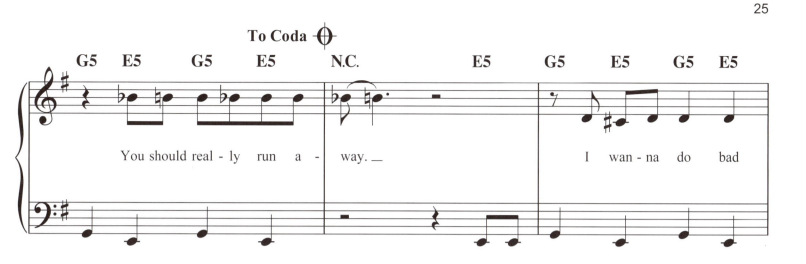

To Coda

You should real-ly run a - way. __ I wan-na do bad

things to you. I wan-na make you yell.

I wan-na do bad things to you. Don't wan-na treat you well. __

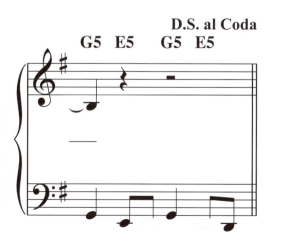

D.S. al Coda

__

CODA

way. __ Oth - er peo-ple would have

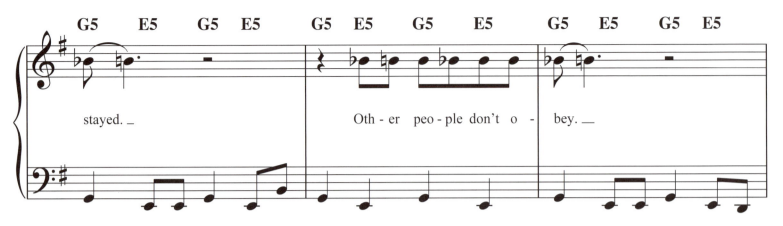

stayed. ___ Oth - er peo - ple don't o - bey. ___

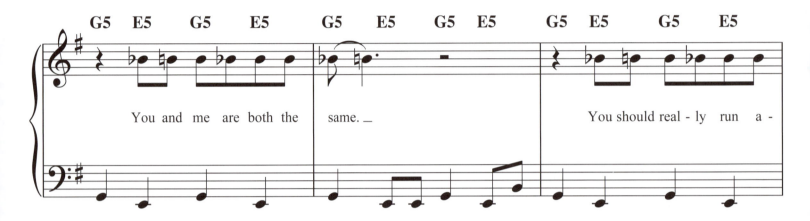

You and me are both the same. ___ You should real - ly run a -

way. ___ Bad things.

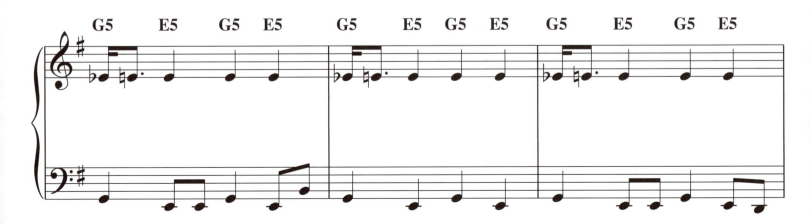

GOLDWING

Words and Music by BILLIE EILISH O'CONNELL
and FINNEAS O'CONNELL

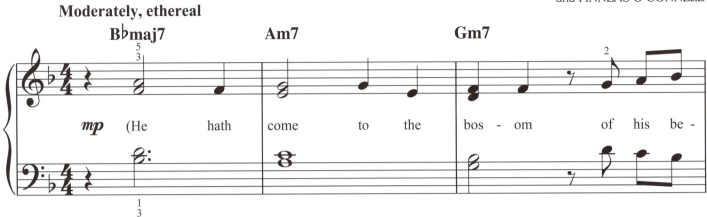

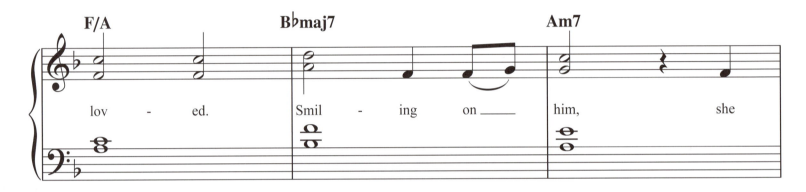

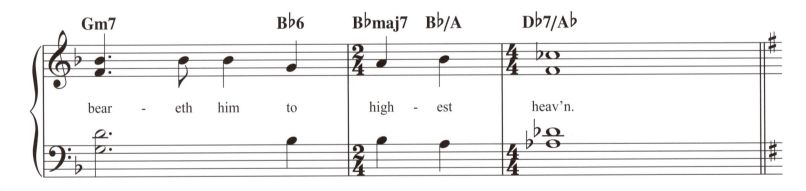

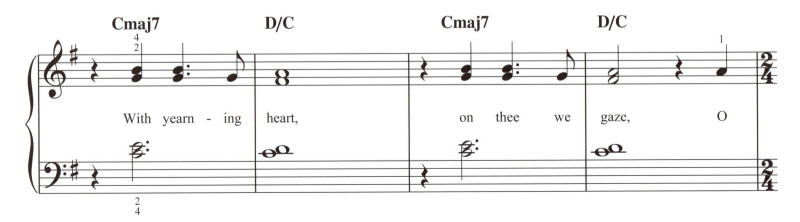

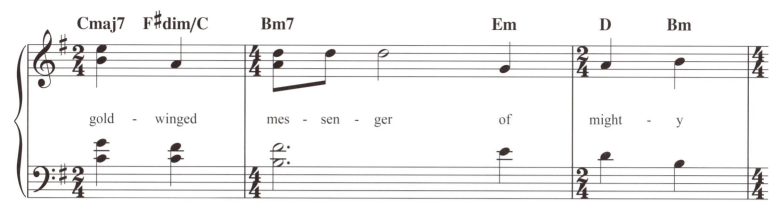

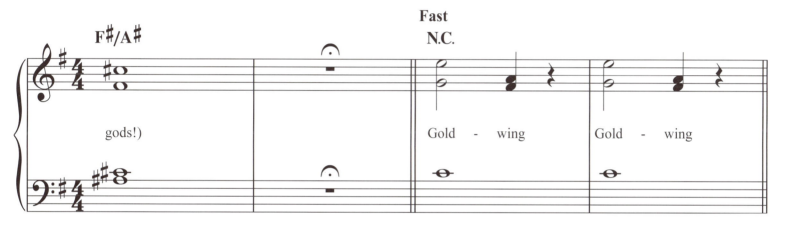

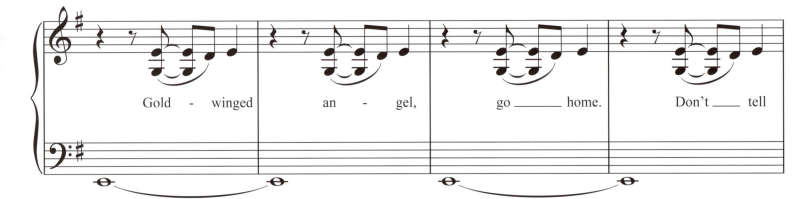

Gold - winged an - gel, go ____ home. Don't ____ tell

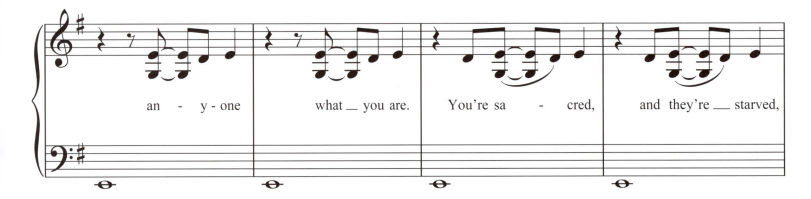

an - y - one what __ you are. You're sa - cred, and they're __ starved,

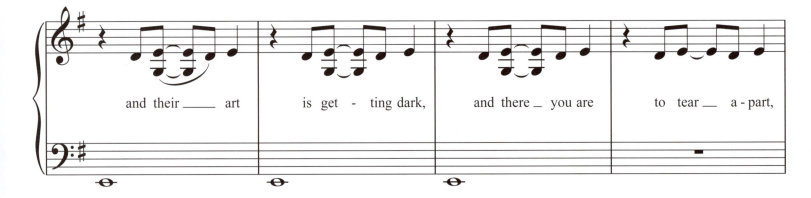

and their ____ art is get - ting dark, and there __ you are to tear __ a - part,

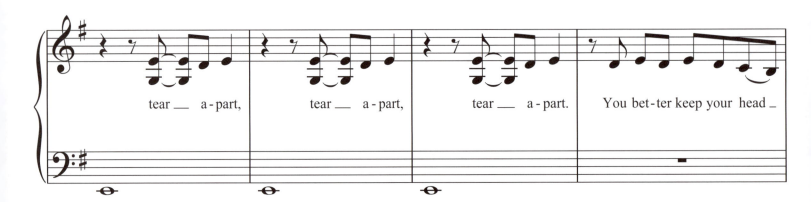

tear __ a - part, tear __ a - part, tear __ a - part. You bet - ter keep your head __

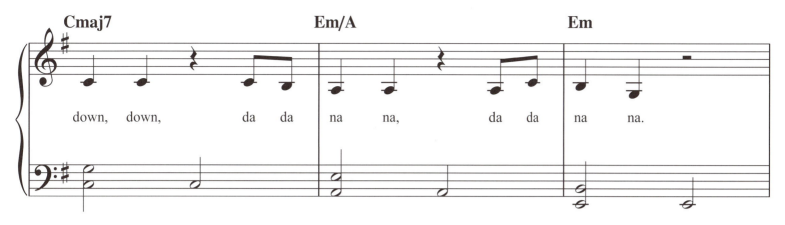

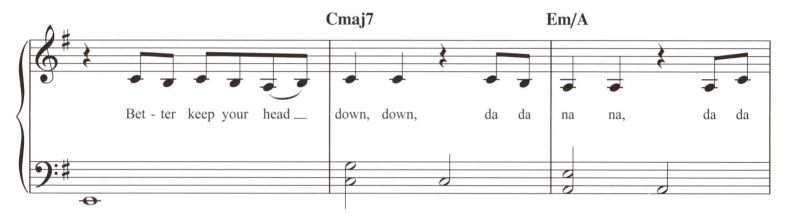

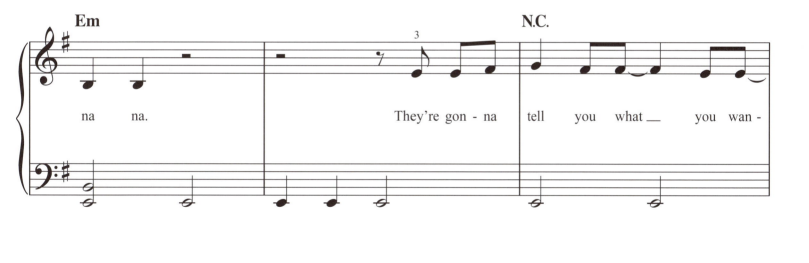

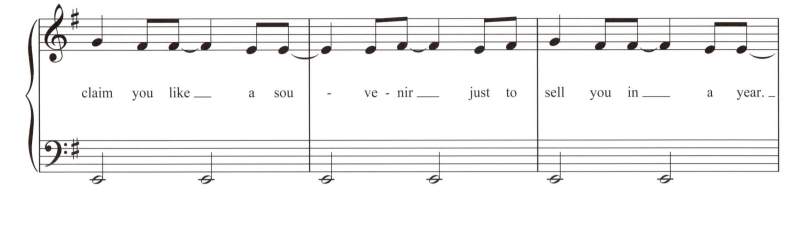

claim you like ___ a sou - ve - nir ___ just to sell you in ___ a year. ___

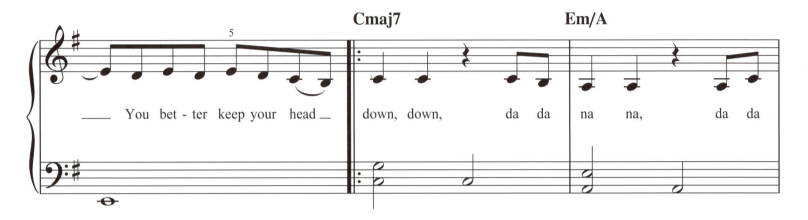

Cmaj7　　　　　**Em/A**

___ You bet - ter keep your head ___ down, down, da da na na, da da

Em　　　　　**Cmaj7**　　　　　**Em/A**

na na.　　　Keep your head down, down, da da na na, da da

Em

na na.

1.
Bet - ter keep your head ___

2.
That's good.

LOST CAUSE

Words and Music by BILLIE EILISH O'CONNELL
and FINNEAS O'CONNELL

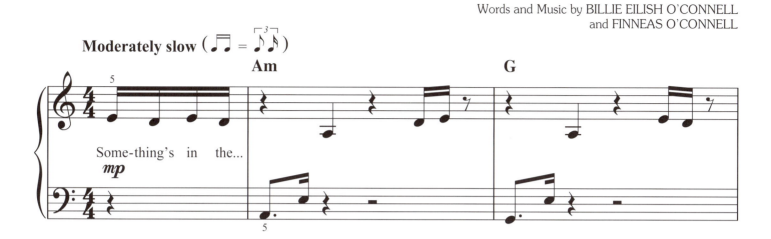

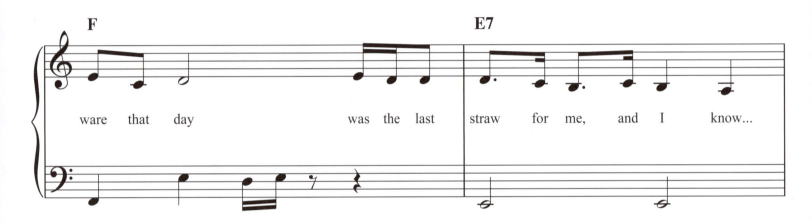

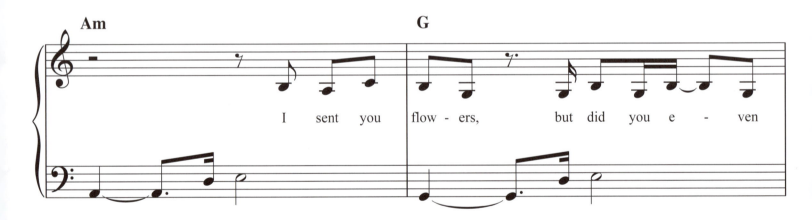

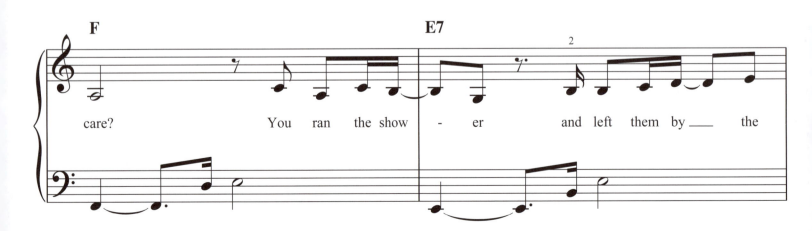

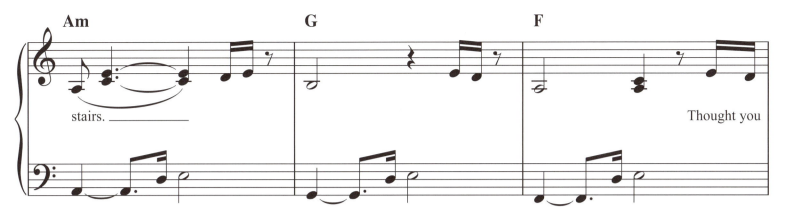

stairs. _____ Thought you

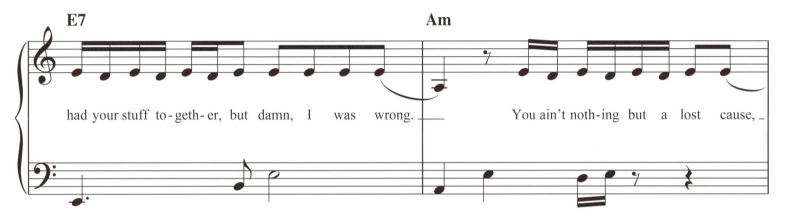

had your stuff to-geth-er, but damn, I was wrong. ___ You ain't noth-ing but a lost cause, __

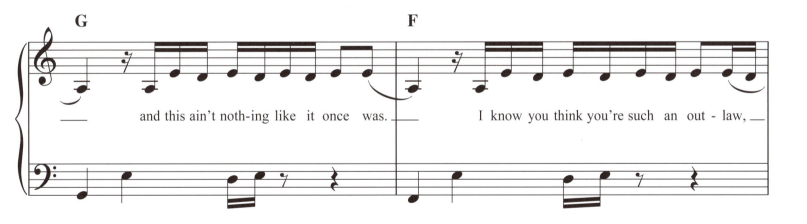

___ and this ain't noth-ing like it once was. ___ I know you think you're such an out-law, __

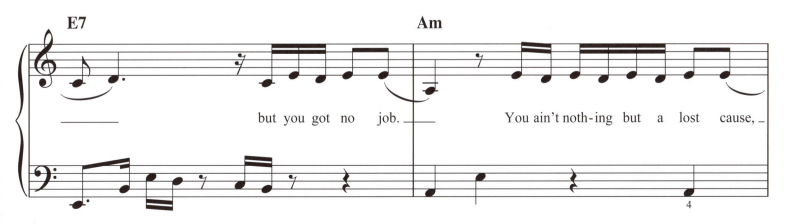

___ but you got no job. ___ You ain't noth-ing but a lost cause, __

4

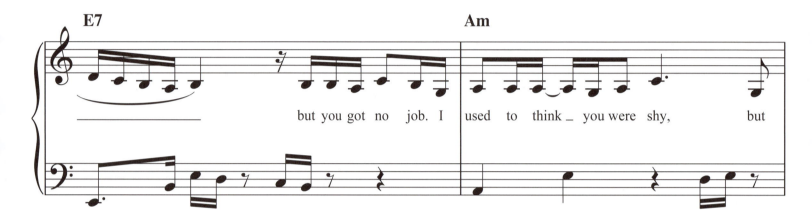

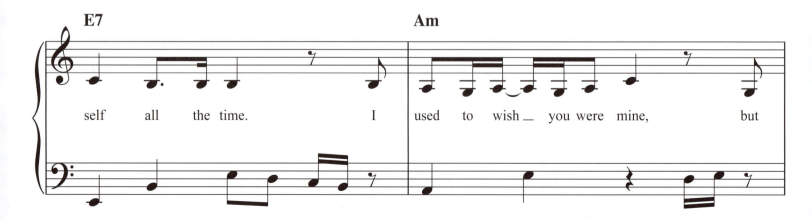

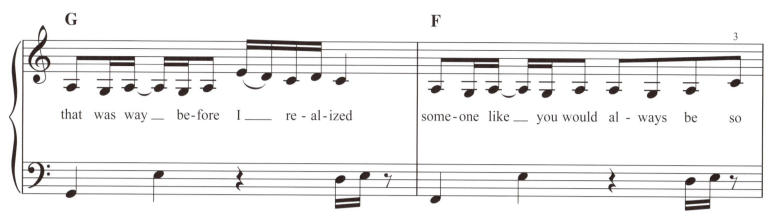

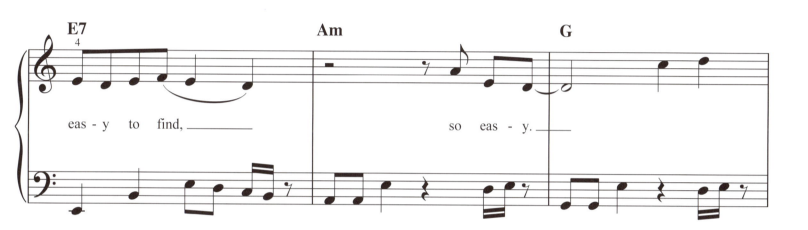

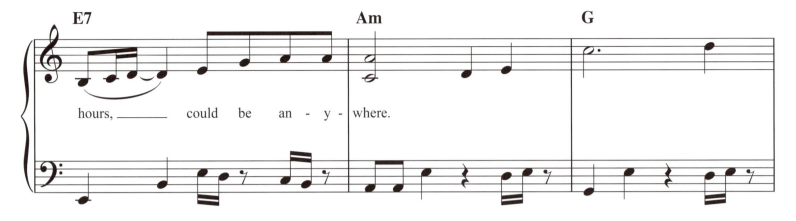

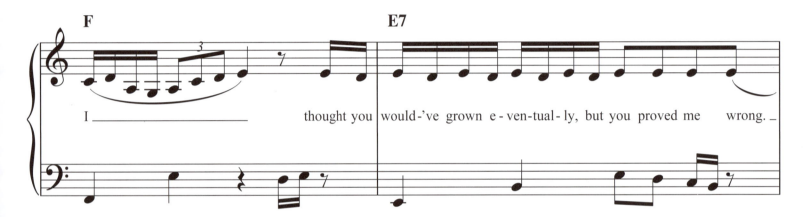

You ain't noth-ing but a lost cause, and this ain't noth-ing like it once was.

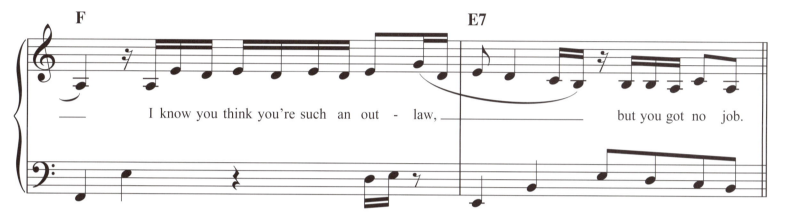

I know you think you're such an out - law, but you got no job.

HALLEY'S COMET

Words and Music by BILLIE EILISH O'CONNELL
and FINNEAS O'CONNELL

I don't want it, and I don't want to want you. But

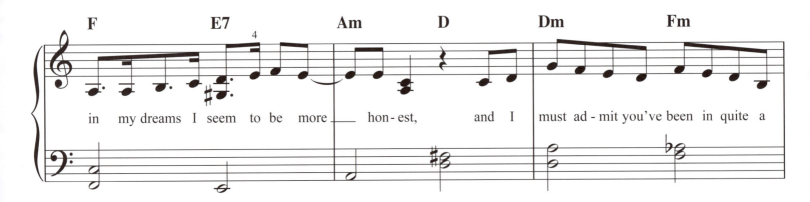

in my dreams I seem to be more ___ hon-est, and I must ad-mit you've been in quite a

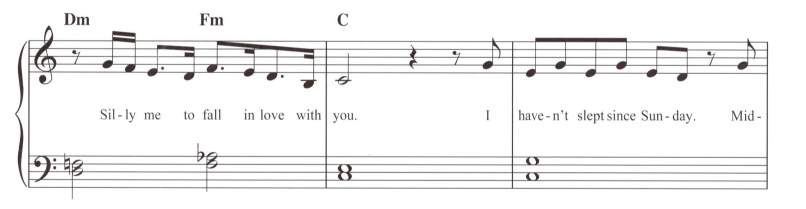

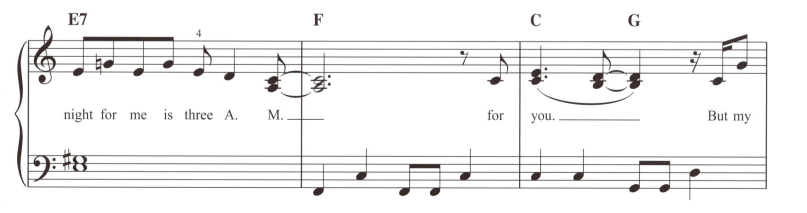

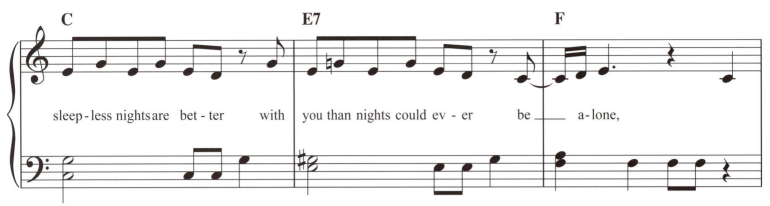

sleep-less nights are bet-ter with you than nights could ev-er be ____ a-lone,

ooh. _____ I was good at feel-in' noth-in', now I'm hope ____ less.

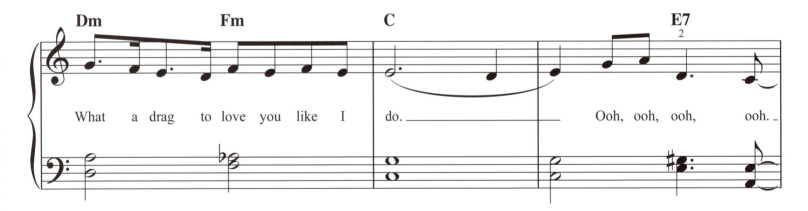

What a drag to love you like I do. _____ Ooh, ooh, ooh, ooh. _

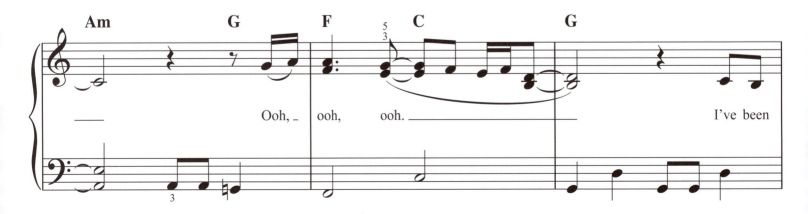

____ Ooh, _ ooh, ooh. _____ I've been

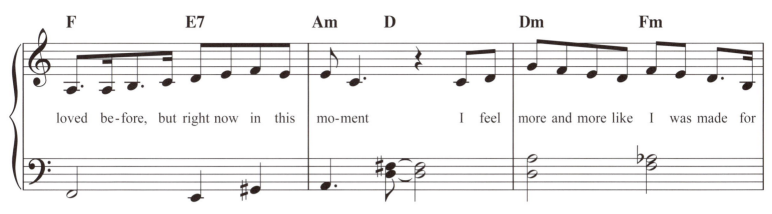

loved be-fore, but right now in this mo-ment I feel more and more like I was made for

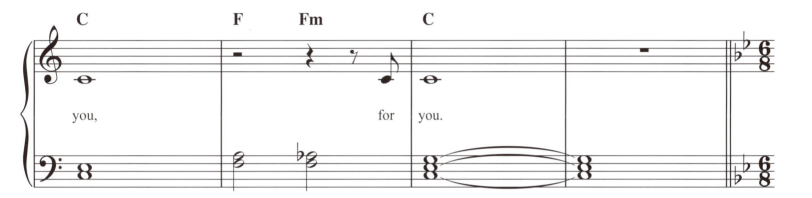

you, for you.

Slower

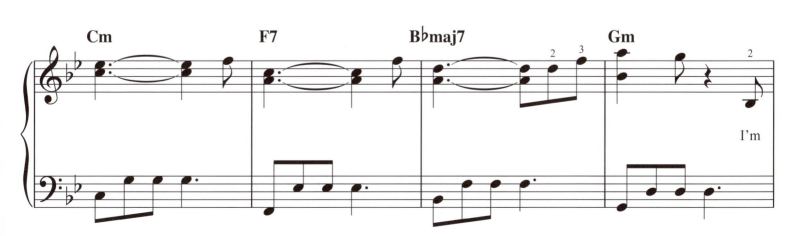

I'm

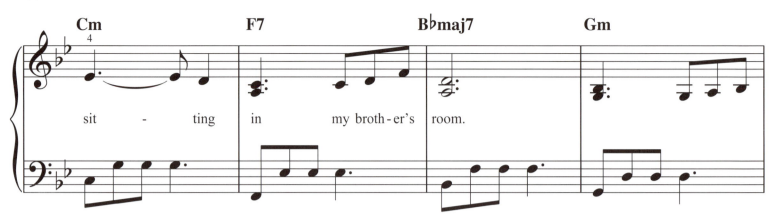

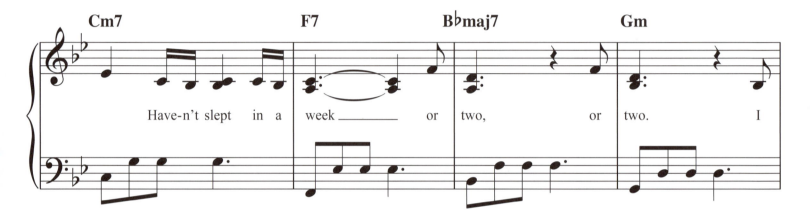

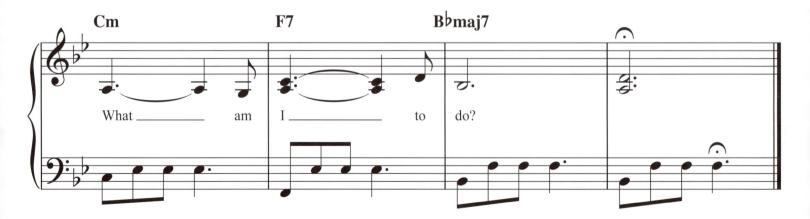

EVERYBODY DIES

Words and Music by BILLIE EILISH O'CONNELL
and FINNEAS O'CONNELL

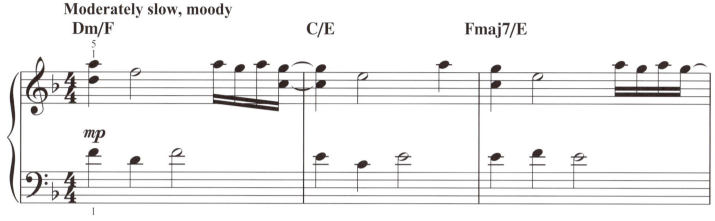

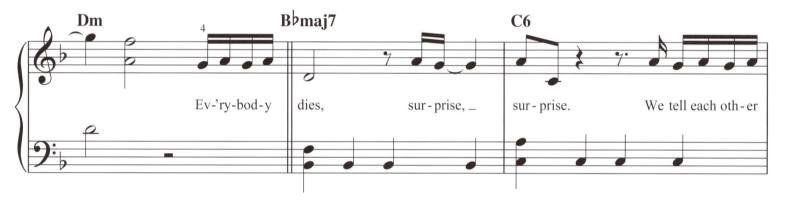

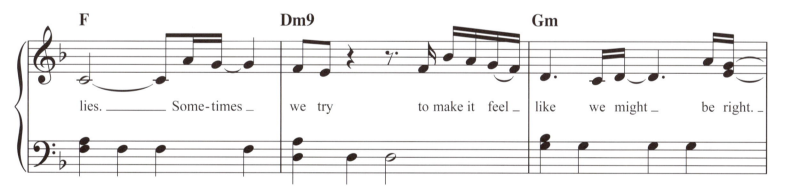

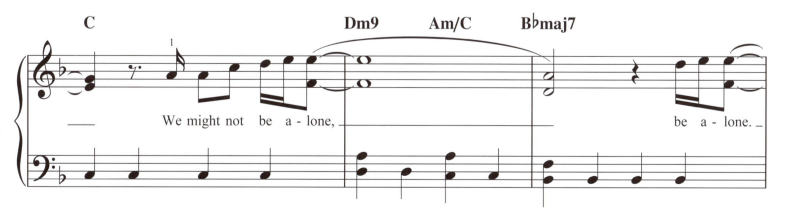

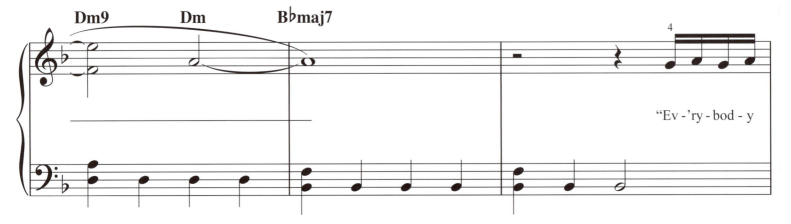

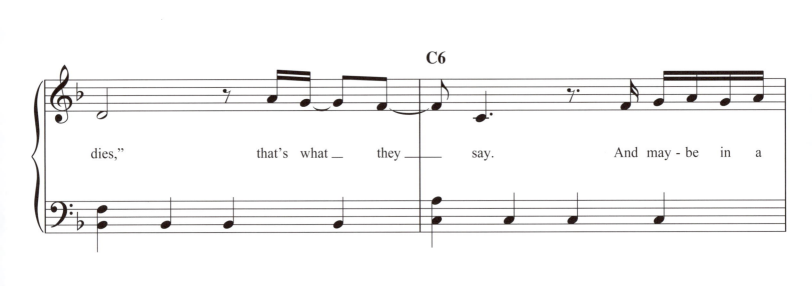

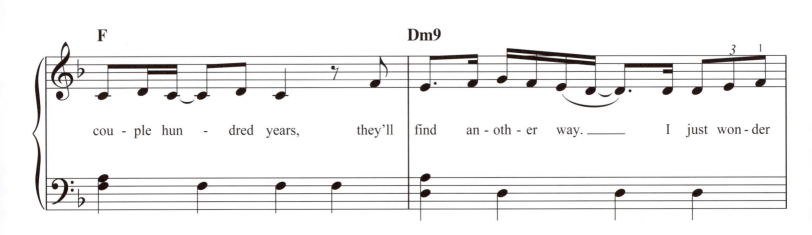

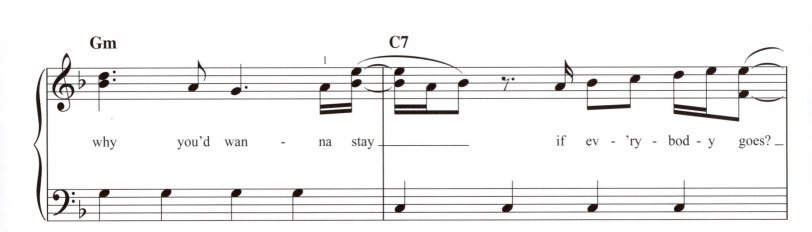

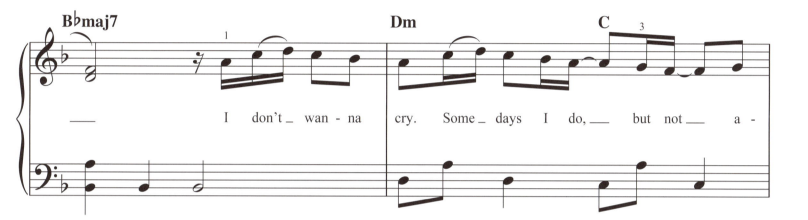

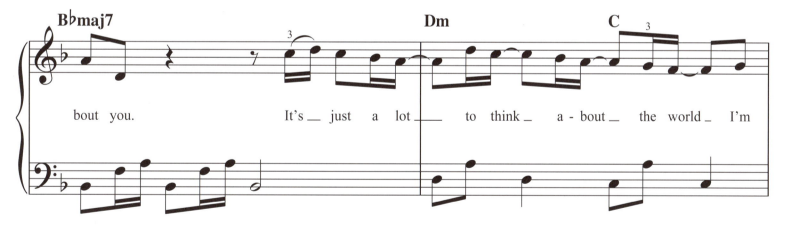

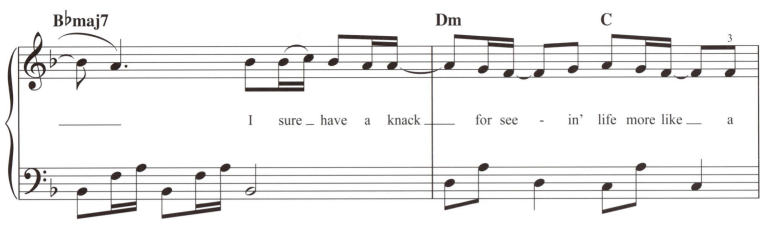

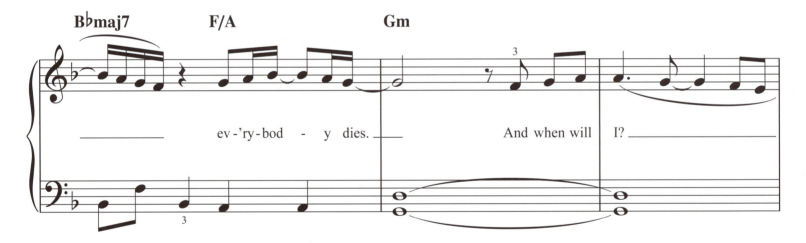

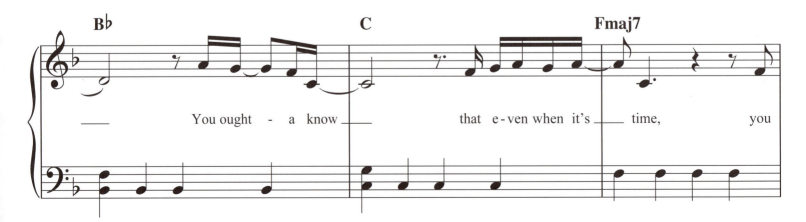

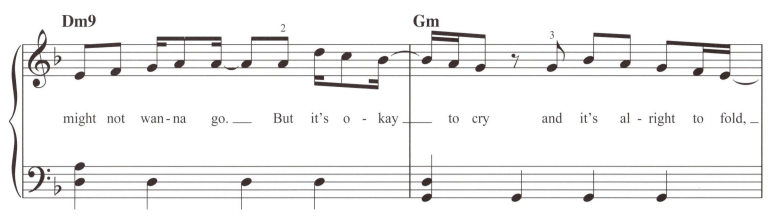

might not wan-na go. ___ But it's o - kay ___ to cry and it's al - right to fold, ___

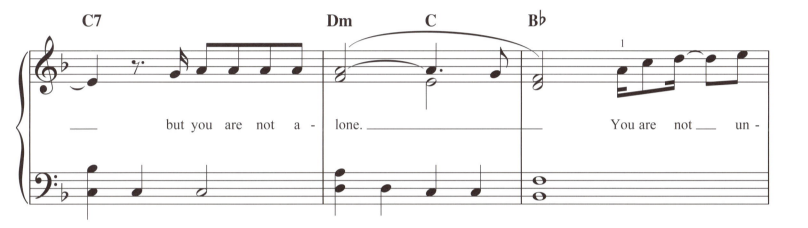

___ but you are not a - lone. ___ You are not ___ un -

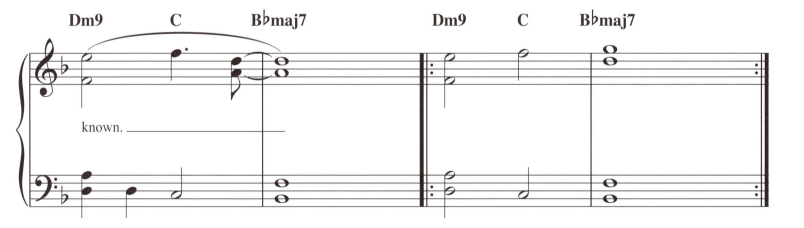

known. ___

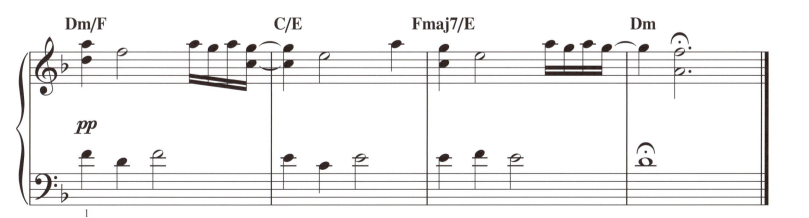

OVERHEATED

Words and Music by BILLIE EILISH O'CONNELL
and FINNEAS O'CONNELL

Moderate Pop

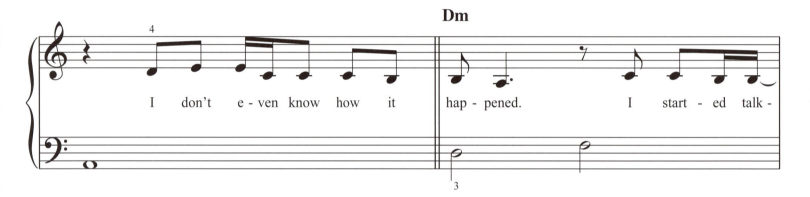

I don't e-ven know how it hap-pened. I start-ed talk-

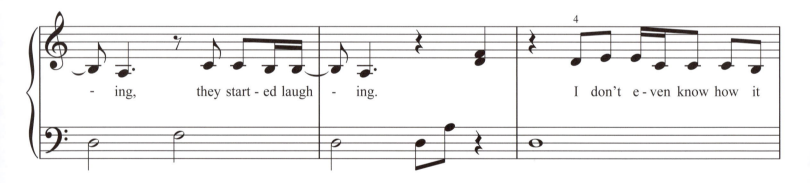

-ing, they start-ed laugh-ing. I don't e-ven know how it

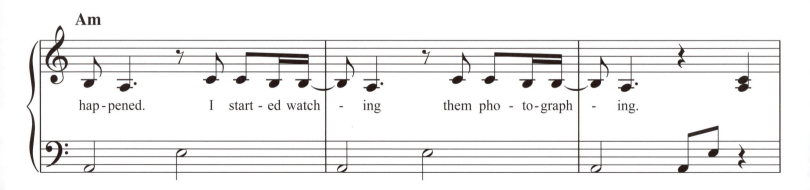

hap-pened. I start-ed watch-ing them pho-to-graph-ing.

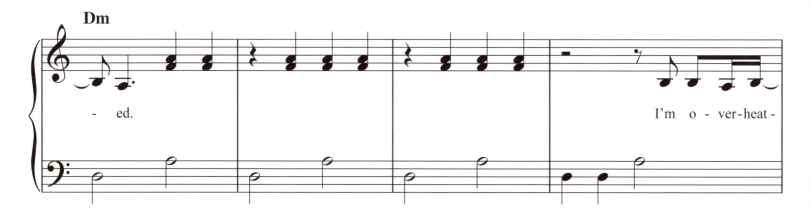

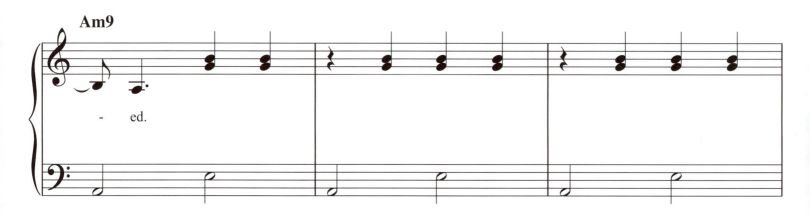

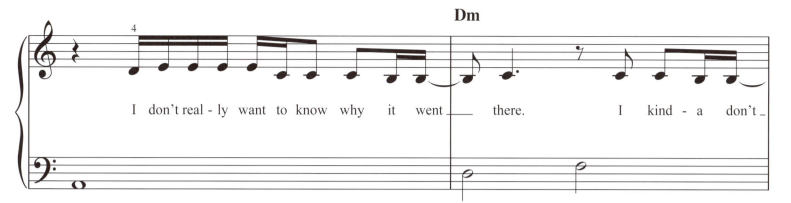

I don't real - ly want to know why it went ___ there. I kind - a don't ___

___ care. You want to kill ___ me? You want to hurt ___ me? Stop be - ing flirt -

- y. It's kind - a work - ing.

Did you real - ly think "This is the right thing to do?" Is it

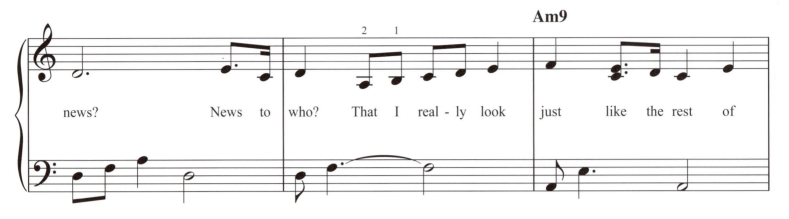

news?　　　News to who?　That I real - ly look　just　like the rest of

you. _____　　　　　　　　　　　　　　　I'm o - ver-heat -

- ed,　　can't be de-feat - ed,　　can't be de-let - ed,　　can't un - be - lieve __

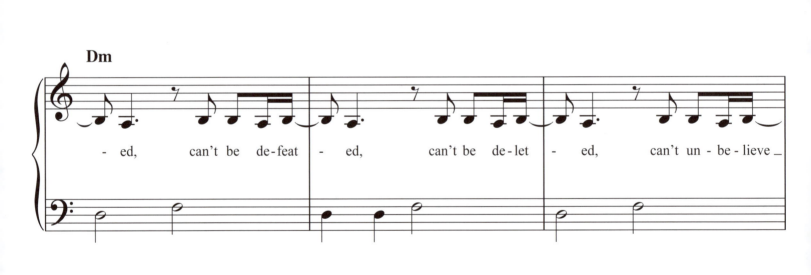

____ it.　I'm o - ver-heat - ed,　can't be de-feat - ed,　can't be de-let -

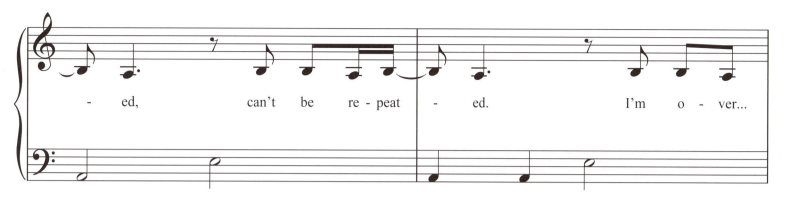

- ed, can't be re - peat - ed. I'm o - ver...

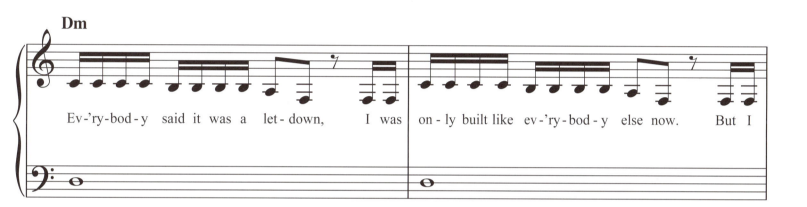

Dm Ev-'ry-bod-y said it was a let-down, I was on - ly built like ev-'ry-bod - y else now. But I

did-n't get a sur-ger - y to help out 'cause I'm not a-bout to re - de-sign my-self, now, am I?

Am

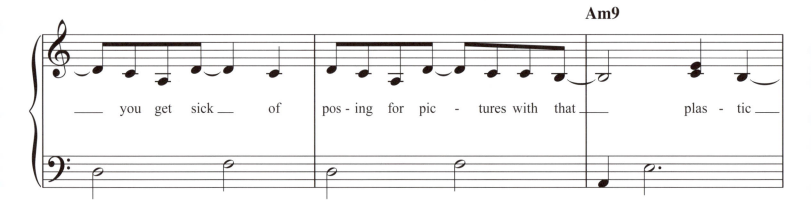

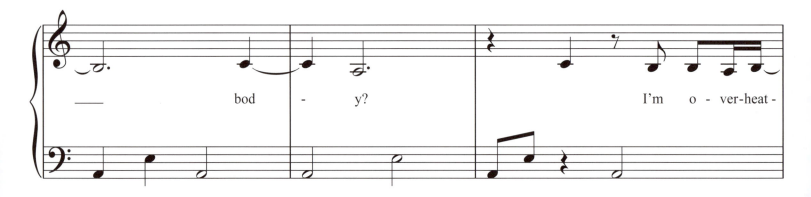

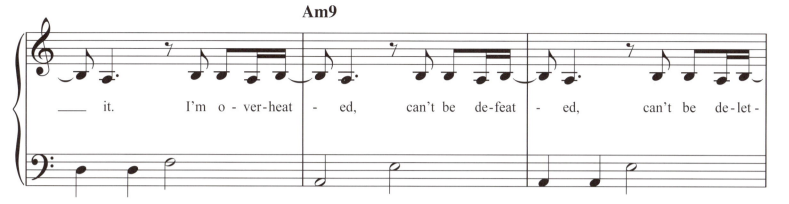

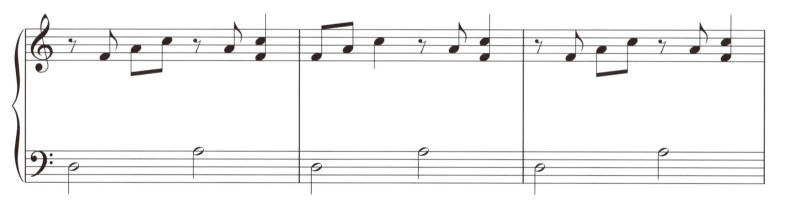

YOUR POWER

Words and Music by BILLIE EILISH O'CONNELL
and FINNEAS O'CONNELL

Moderately fast

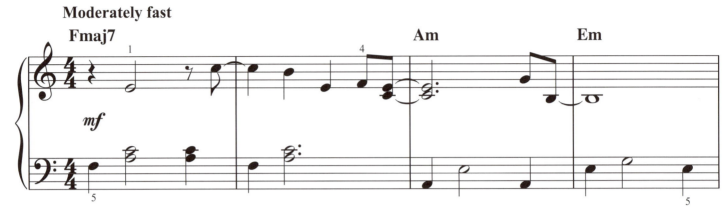

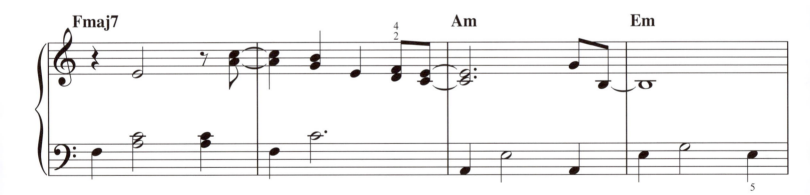

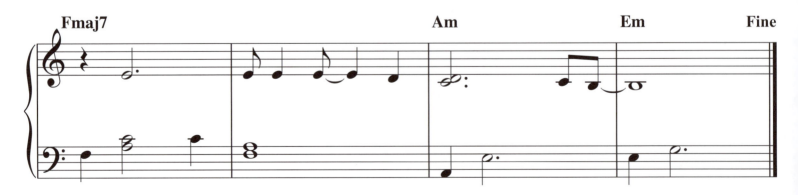

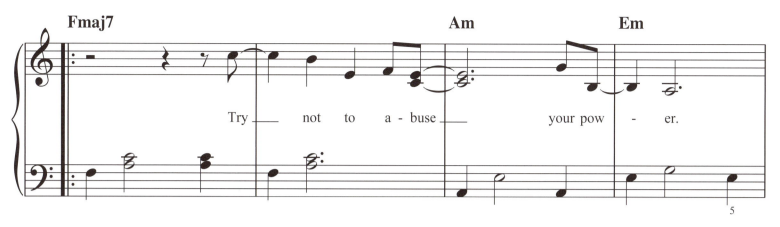

Try ___ not to a - buse ___ your pow - er.

I know ___ we did - n't choose ___ to change.

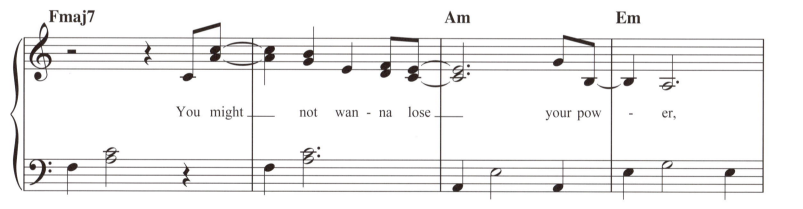

You might ___ not wan - na lose ___ your pow - er,

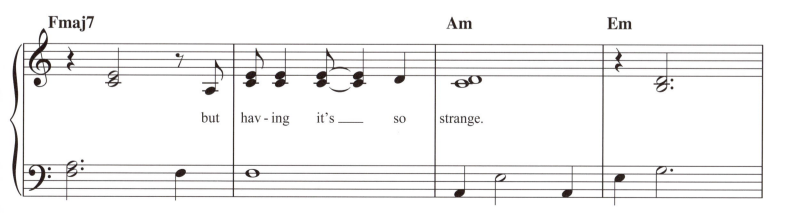

but hav - ing it's ___ so strange.

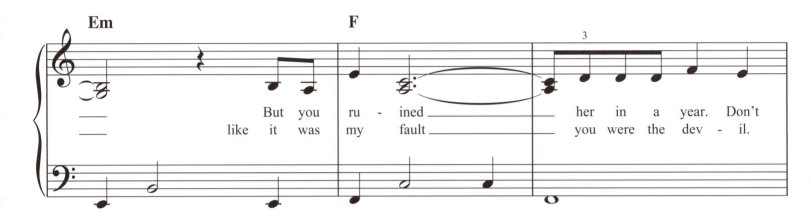

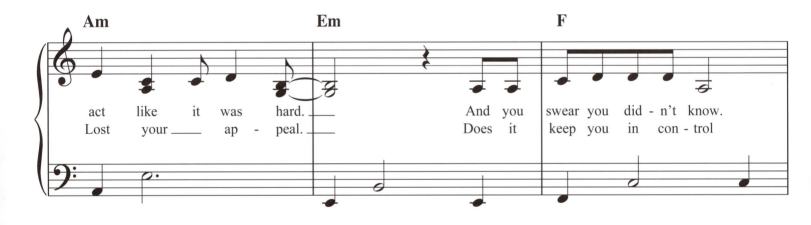

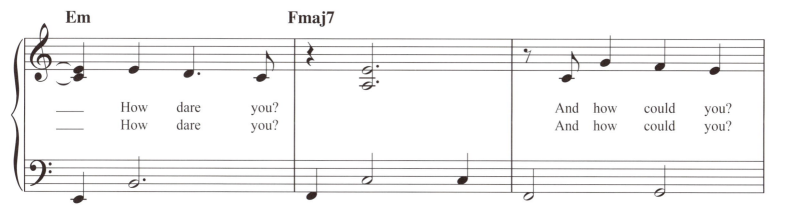

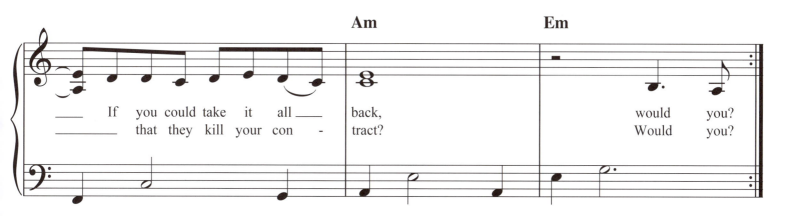

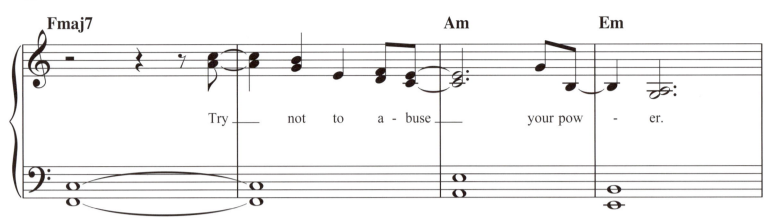

Try ___ not to a - buse ___ your pow - er.

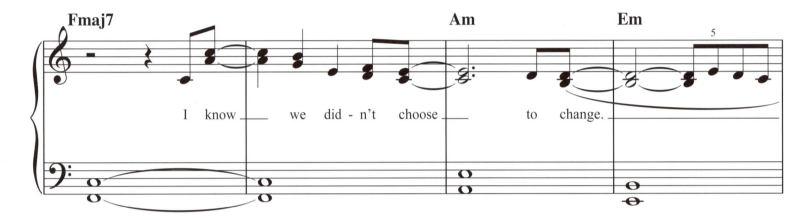

I know ___ we did - n't choose ___ to change. ___

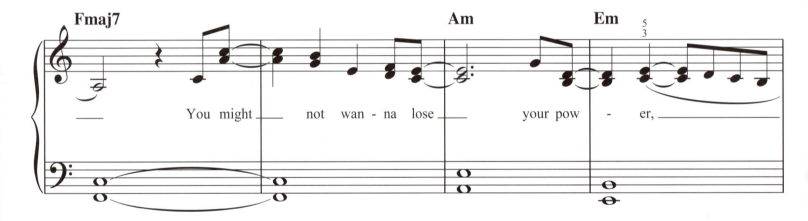

___ You might ___ not wan - na lose ___ your pow - er, ___

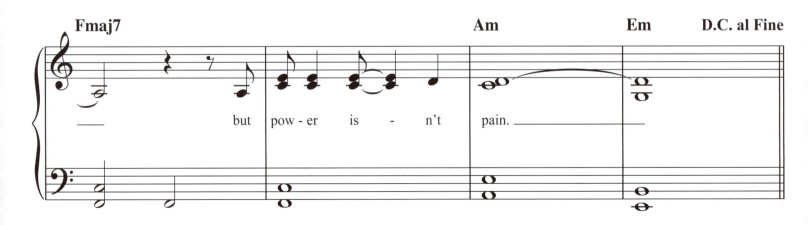

___ but pow - er is - n't pain. ___

MALE FANTASY

Words and Music by BILLIE EILISH O'CONNELL
and FINNEAS O'CONNELL

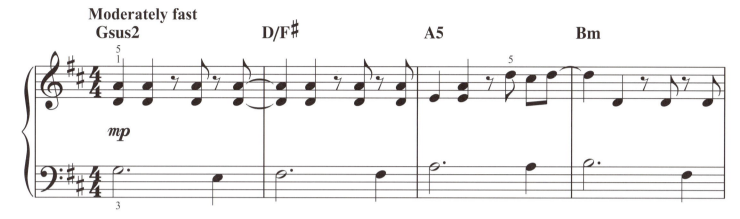

Home a - lone, try - in' not to eat. Dis - tract my - self

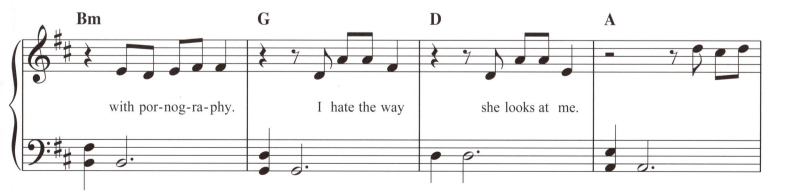

with por-nog-ra-phy. I hate the way she looks at me.

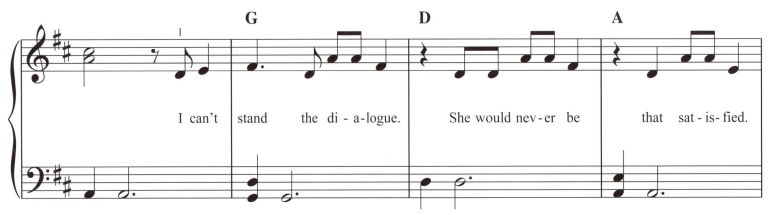

I can't stand the di - a-logue. She would nev-er be that sat - is-fied.

It's a male __ fan - ta - sy. I'm go - in' back to ther - a - py.

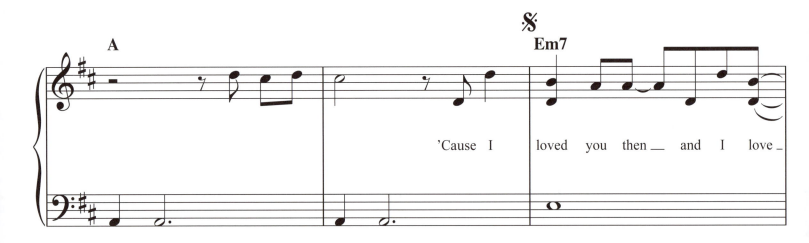

'Cause I loved you then __ and I love __

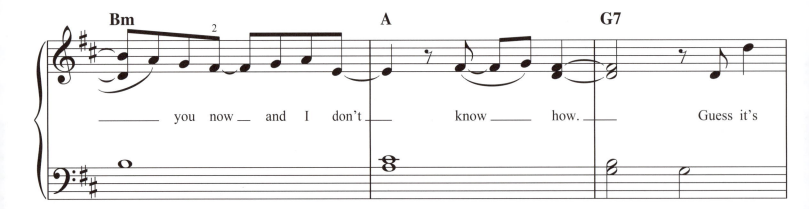

__ you now __ and I don't __ know __ how. __ Guess it's

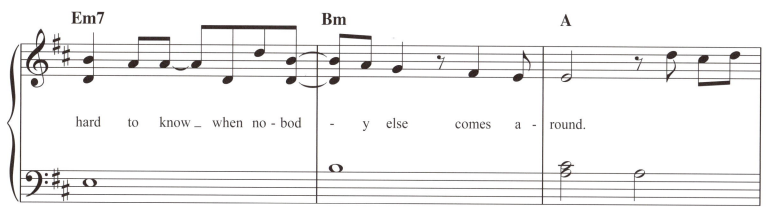

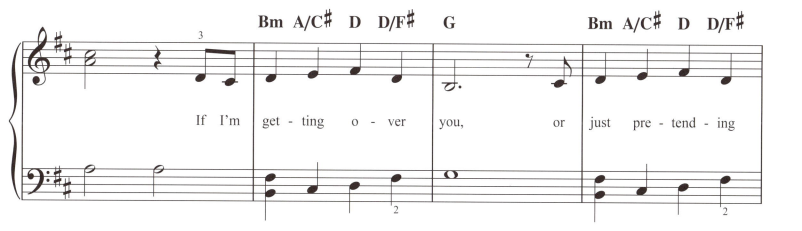

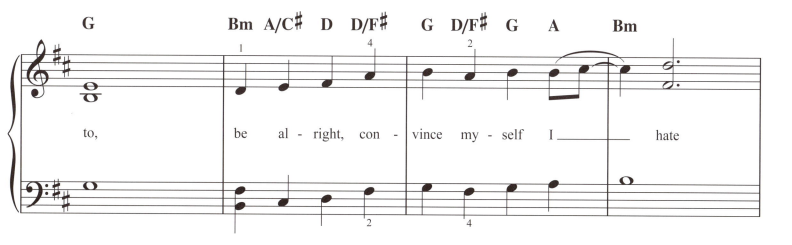

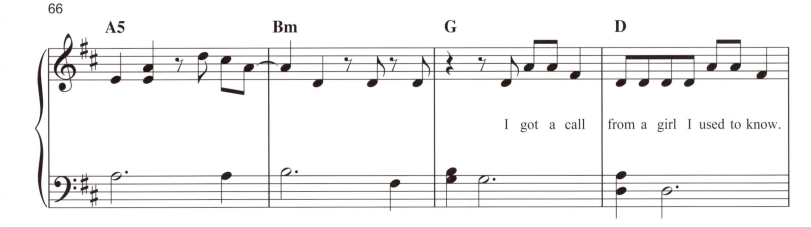

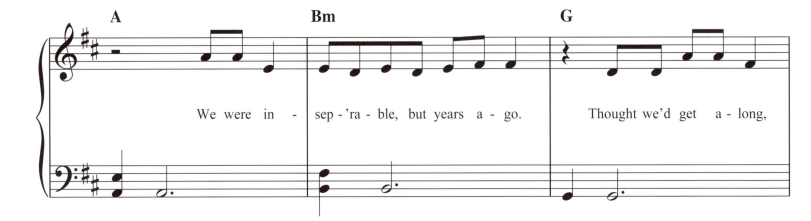

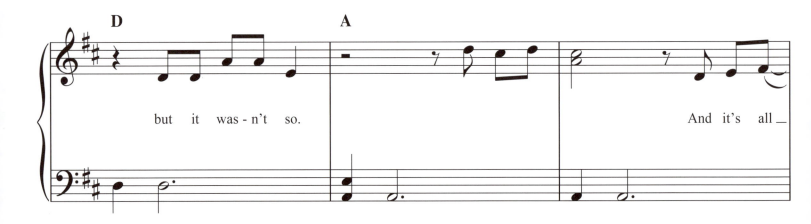

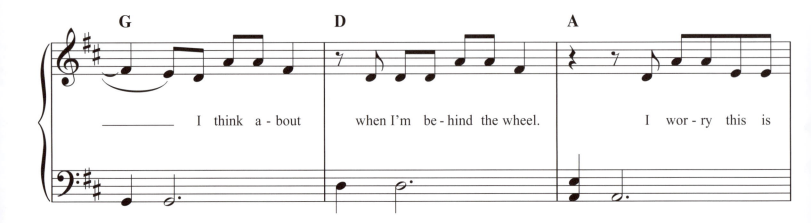

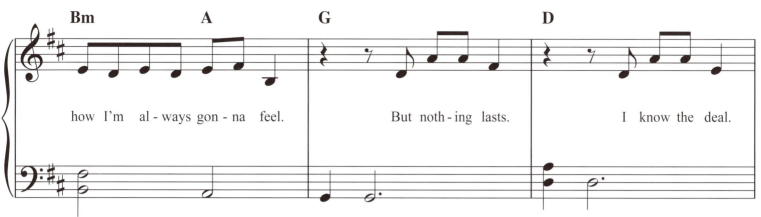

Bm · **A** · **G** · **D**

how I'm al-ways gon-na feel. But noth-ing lasts. I know the deal.

A · D.S. al Coda

But I

CODA

Bm A/C# D D/F#

Can't get o-ver __

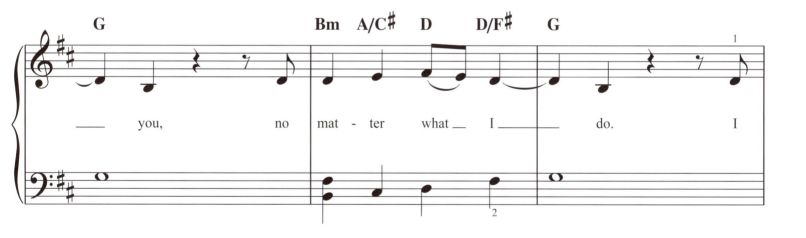

G · **Bm A/C# D D/F# G**

__ you, no mat-ter what __ I ____ do. I

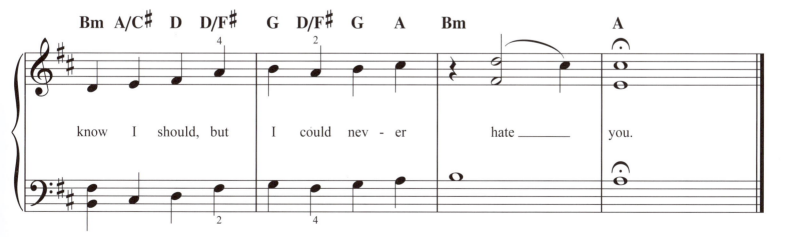

Bm A/C# D D/F# G D/F# G A Bm · **A**

know I should, but I could nev-er hate _____ you.

THEREFORE I AM

Words and Music by BILLIE EILISH O'CONNELL
and FINNEAS O'CONNELL

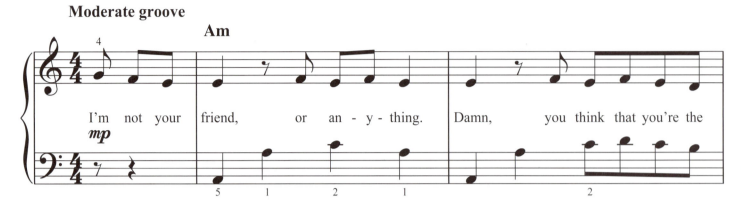

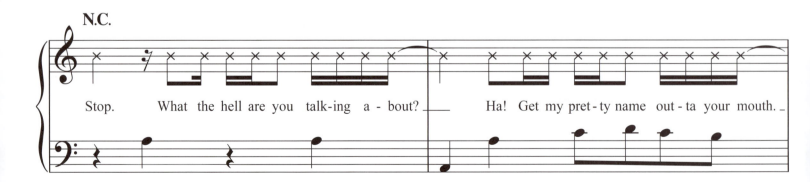

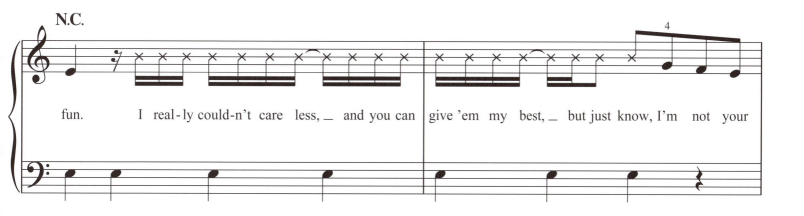

friend, or an-y-thing. Damn, you think that you're the man. ___ I think, there-fore I

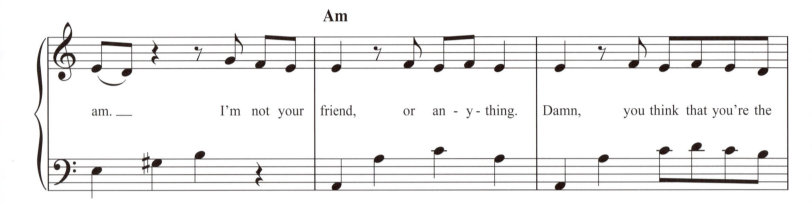

am. ___ I'm not your friend, or an-y-thing. Damn, you think that you're the

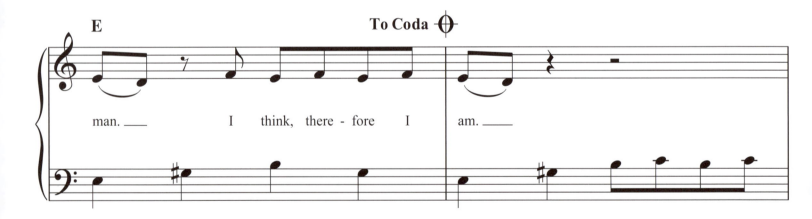

man. ___ I think, there-fore I am. ___

I don't want press to put ___ your name next to mine. ___ We're on dif-f'rent lines, ___ so I

wan-na be nice e-nough __ they don't | call my bluff. __ 'Cause I hate to find __

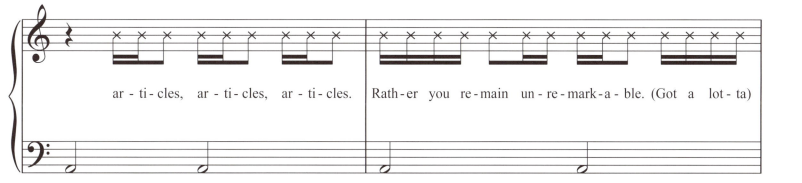

ar-ti-cles, ar-ti-cles, ar-ti-cles. | Rath-er you re-main un-re-mark-a-ble. (Got a lot-ta)

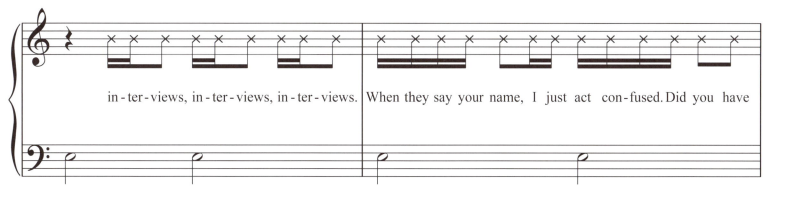

in-ter-views, in-ter-views, in-ter-views. | When they say your name, I just act con-fused. Did you have

D.S. al Coda

fun? *(Spoken:)* *I really couldn't care less, and you can* | *give 'em my best, but just know,* I'm not your

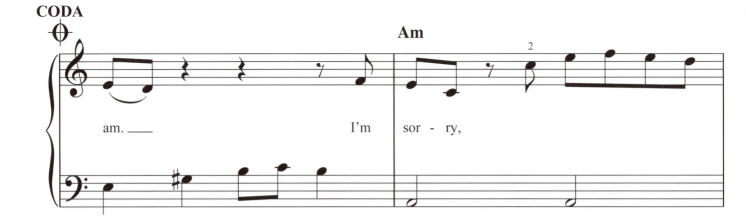

am. ____ I'm sor - ry,

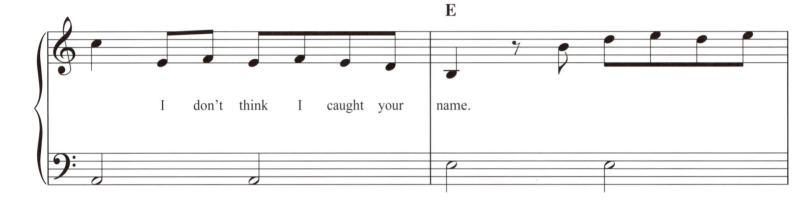

I don't think I caught your name.

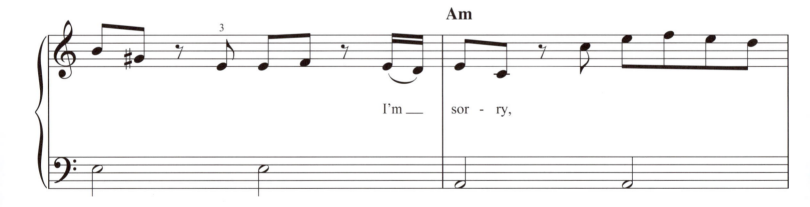

I'm __ sor - ry,

I don't think I caught your name. _____

I'm not your friend, or an-y-thing. Damn, you think that you're the

man. __ I think, there-fore I am. __ I'm not your friend, or an-y-thing.

Damn, you think that you're the man. __ I think, there-fore I am. __

HAPPIER THAN EVER

Words and Music by BILLIE EILISH O'CONNELL
and FINNEAS O'CONNELL

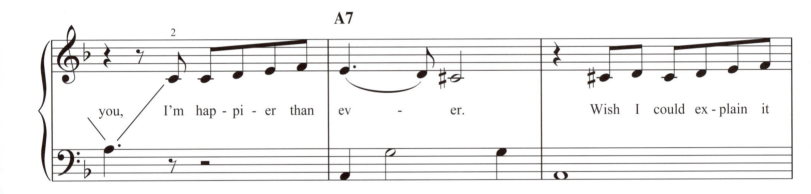

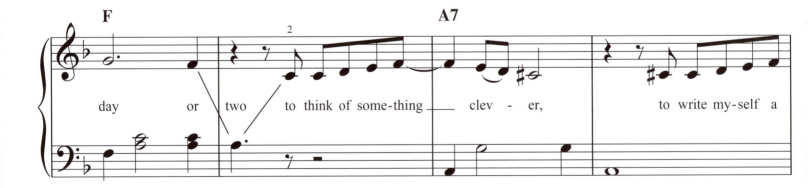

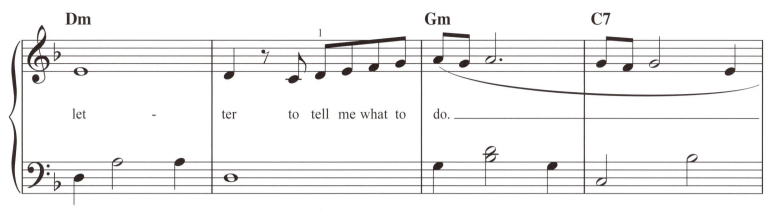

let - ter to tell me what to do. ____

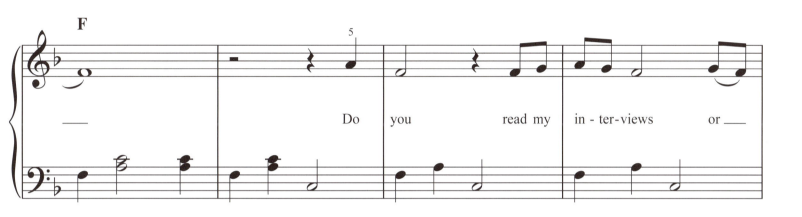

____ Do you read my in - ter-views or ____

do you skip my av - e - nue? When you said you were pass-in' through, was I

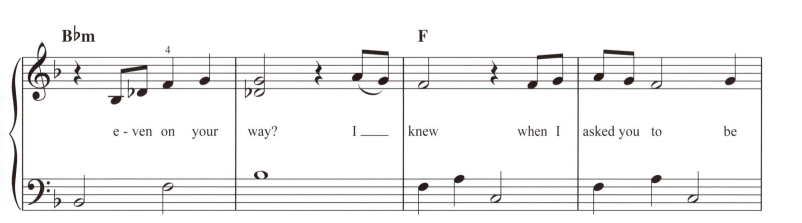

e - ven on your way? I ____ knew when I asked you to be

cool a - bout what I was tell - ing you, you would do the op - po - site of what you

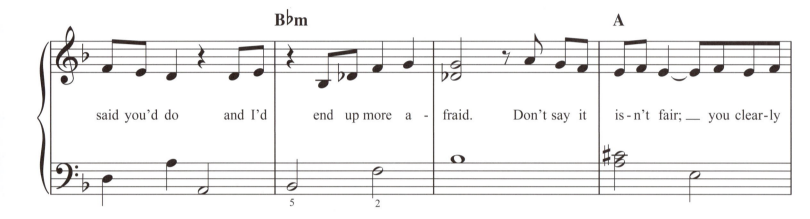

said you'd do and I'd end up more a - fraid. Don't say it is - n't fair; __ you clear - ly

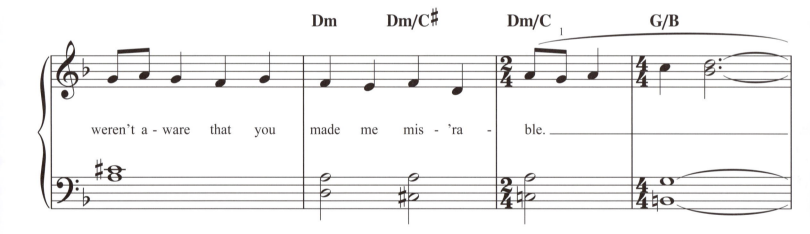

weren't a - ware that you made me mis - 'ra - ble. _____

_____ So, if you real - ly wan - na know, when I'm a - way from

A7 ... **Dm**

you, I'm hap-pi-er than ev - er. Wish I could ex-plain it bet -

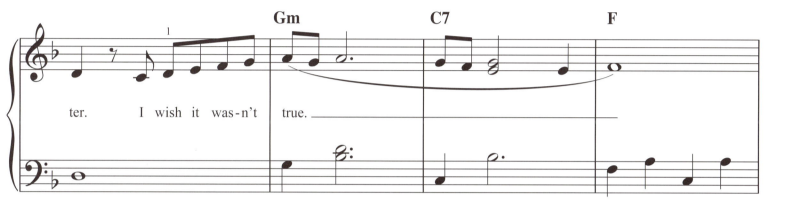

Gm ... **C7** ... **F**

ter. I wish it was-n't true. _____

Moderate Waltz, in 2

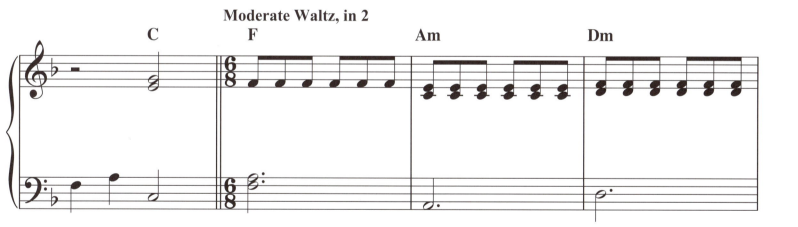

C ... **F** ... **Am** ... **Dm**

B♭ ... **B♭m** ... **F5** ... **A5**

You call me a - gain, ____ drunk in your Benz. __

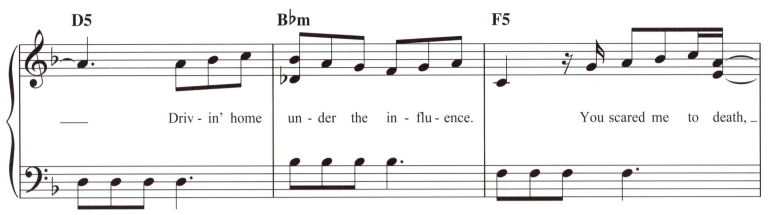

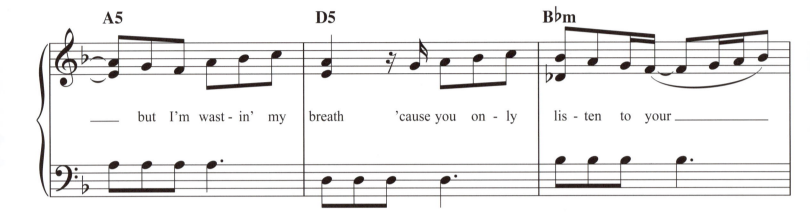

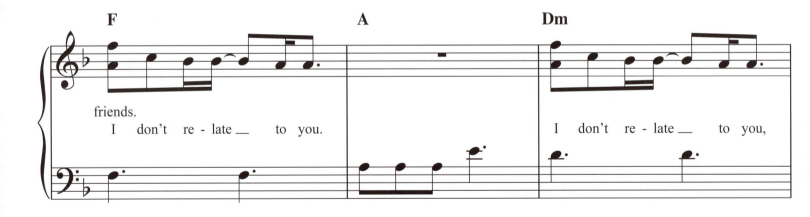

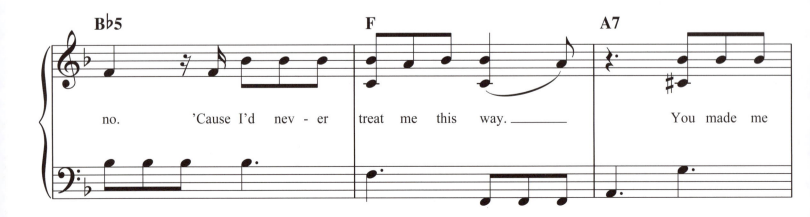

hate this cit - y. And I don't talk shit a-bout you on the

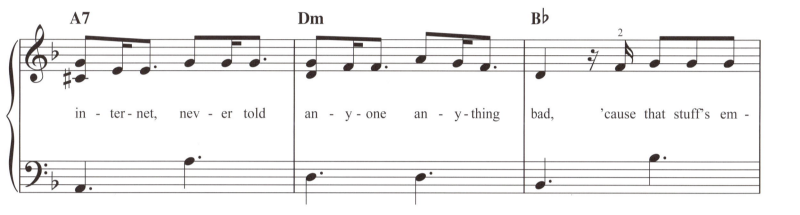

in - ter - net, nev - er told an - y - one an - y - thing bad, 'cause that stuff's em -

bar - rass - ing. You were my ev - 'ry - thing and all that you did was make me _____

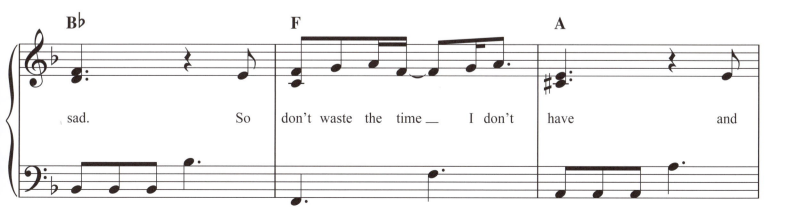

sad. So don't waste the time __ I don't have and

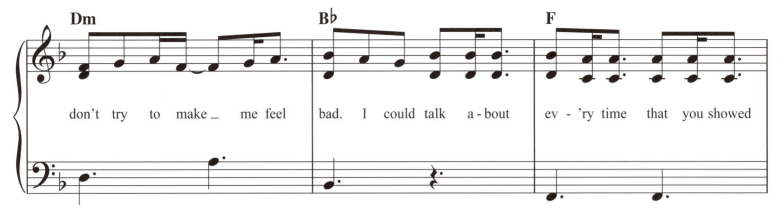

stood.   Made all my mo - ments your   own.

Just   leave me a -   lone. _____

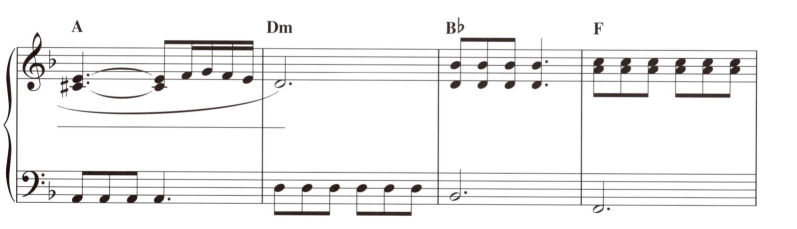

NDA

Words and Music by BILLIE EILISH O'CONNELL
and FINNEAS O'CONNELL

Dark Pop

Did you think I'd show up in a lim-ou-sine? No, had to save my mon-ey for se-cu-ri-ty. Got a

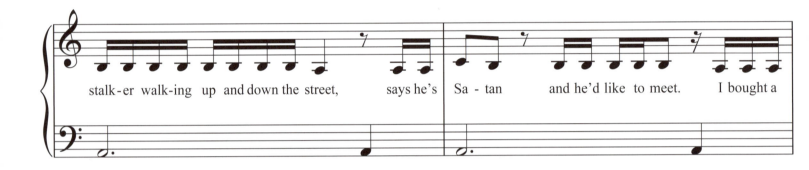

stalk-er walk-ing up and down the street, says he's Sa-tan and he'd like to meet. I bought a

se-cret house when I was sev-en-teen, have-n't had a par-ty since I got the keys. Had a

pret-ty boy o-ver, but he could-n't stay. On his way out I made him sign an N D A.

Yeah, I made him sign an

N D A.

Once was good e-nough 'cause I don't want him hav - ing

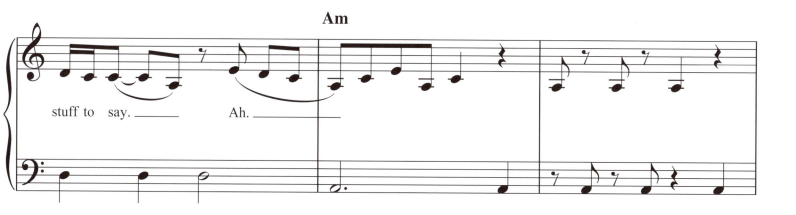

stuff to say. _____ Ah. _____

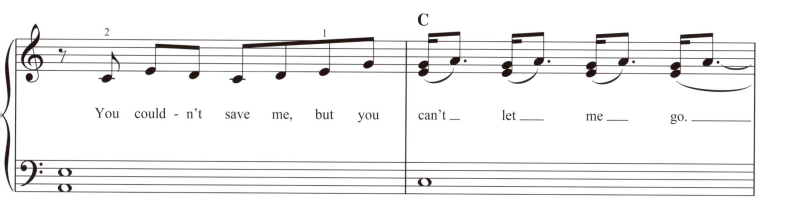

You could - n't save me, but you can't __ let __ me __ go. _____

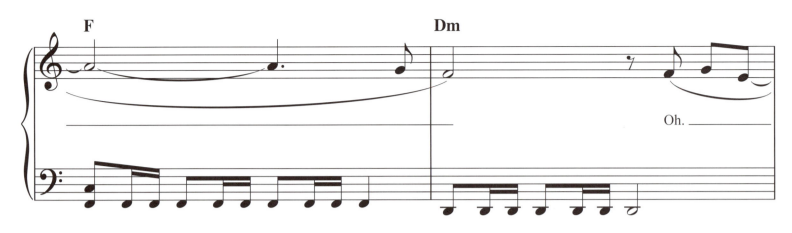

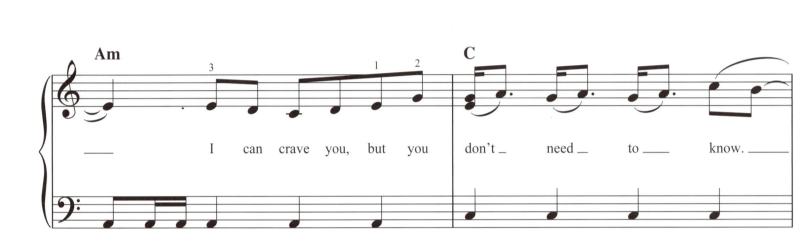

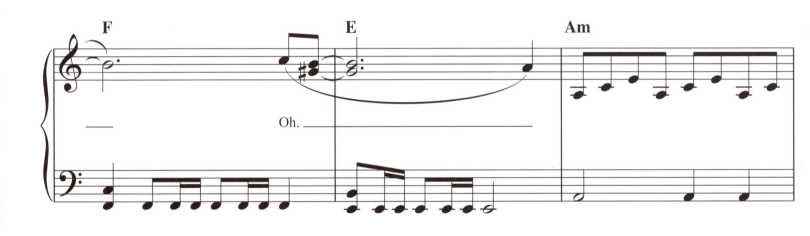

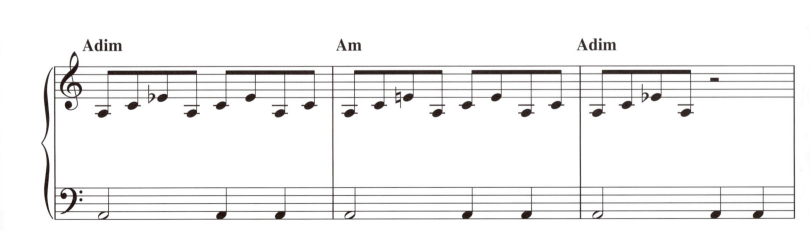

Am

Thir-ty un-der thir-ty for an-oth-er year. I can bare-ly go out-side; I think I hate it here.

May-be I should think a-bout a new ca-reer, some-where in Kau-a'i where I can dis-ap-pear. I've been

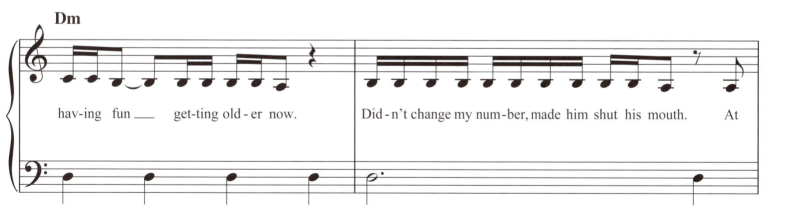

Dm

hav-ing fun ___ get-ting old-er now. Did-n't change my num-ber, made him shut his mouth. At

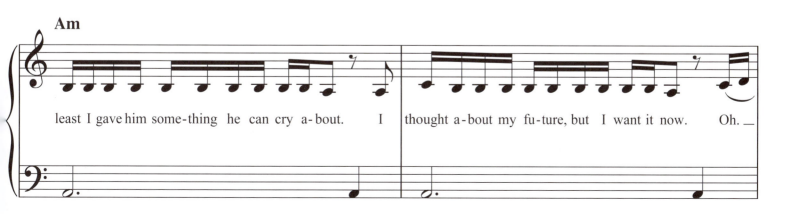

Am

least I gave him some-thing he can cry a-bout. I thought a-bout my fu-ture, but I want it now. Oh. ___

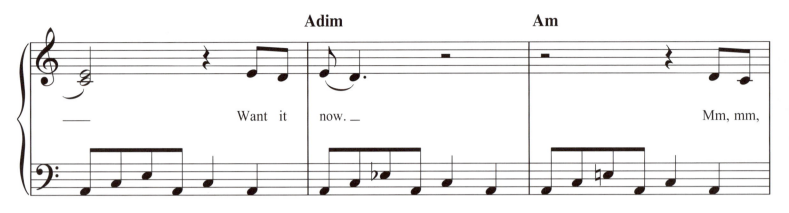

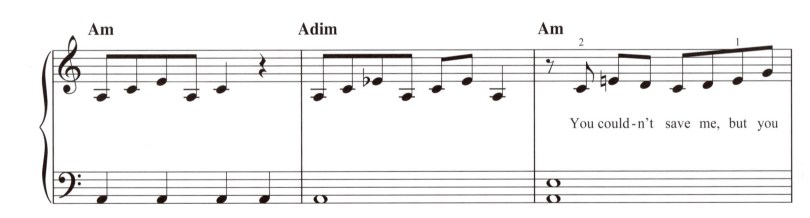

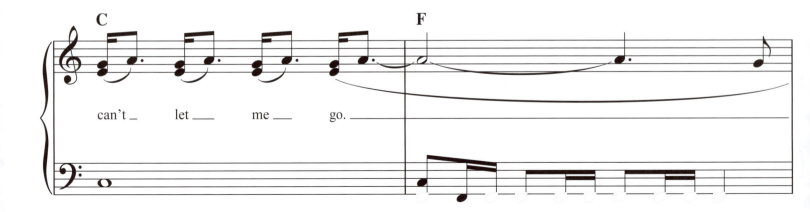

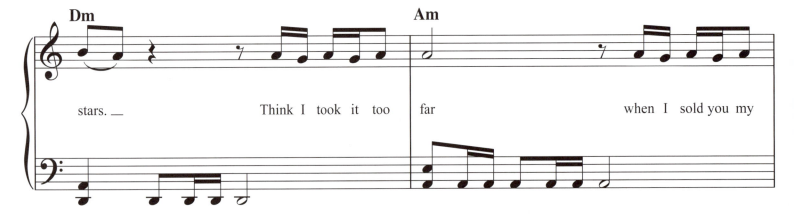

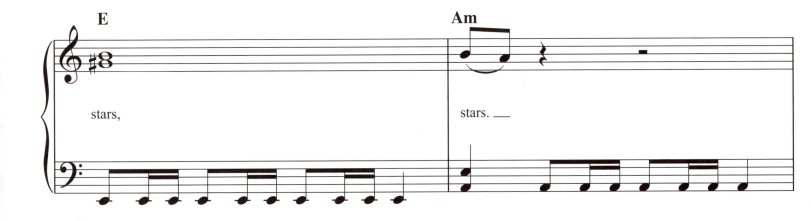

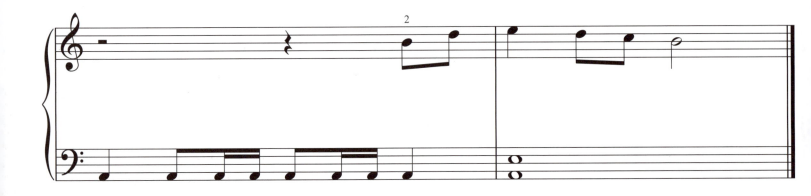